Valerie Preston-Dunlop

# looking at dances

a choreological

perspective on

choreography

NOVERRE
PRESS

First published in 1998 by Verve Publishing,
reprinted in 2000, 2003 and 2006.
This edition first published in 2014 by The Noverre Press,
Southwold House, Isington Road, Binsted, Hampshire GU34 4PH, UK
© 2014 Valerie Preston-Dunlop.
Valerie Preston-Dunlop has asserted her moral right
to be identified as the author of this work.
A catalogue record for this book is available
from the British Library.

ISBN 978-1-906830-70-0

Designed by Glenn Hilling
Illustrations by Angela Geary

Typeset in Joanna and Trade Gothic

# acknowledgements

I am deeply indebted to the choreography mentor Dorothy Madden for her painstaking readings of this text as it emerged. Her critical eye and editing skills have been invaluable as well as making writing the book an enjoyable collaboration.

I thank most warmly the dancers and choreographers with whom I have worked. The Landelijk Centrum voor Amateur Dans has been especially supportive of my courses and relectures with Dutch dance people over some ten years and have commissioned the Dutch edition of this text. The ordering of the content arose partially out of the practical seminars given in the Netherlands under their sponsorship and also from my postgraduate courses at the Laban Centre in London. Stimulating debate with the faculty from all branches of the dance domain who work there have nudged me into articulating what I mean. Comments on the text from my fellow practical scholar Ana Sanchez-Colberg were especially welcome.

The copious attendance at rehearsals that I undertook for the book "Dance Words" gave me opportunity to witness company and independent artists at work, too many to name. I value their willing co-operation unreservedly. The methods of many are referred to in this text.

My thanks to Stine Nilsen and Susannah West, dancers from Transitions Dance Company, and Frederick Curry and Juliano Periera, who acted as models for Angela Geary whose drawings enliven the text and to Rapahael Akopian Schupp who made contact with dance libraries in the Netherlands on my behalf.

Special thanks to Glenn Hilling for his appreciation of my concept for the text and his imaginative design of the book and treatment of Angela's drawings.

# contents

# introduction
## to a choreological perspective

It goes almost without saying that writing a book about dance practice without dance there in front of you to refer to is destined to fail. It is certainly like trying to get over a very high wall with no ladder. But I am prepared to try to climb. Movement described in words is awful. It is, after all, indescribable as is the smell of a rose and the taste of a good wine. But there are things to be said which I know can empower dance people and, notwithstanding the hazards, the problems and the inevitable shortcomings, I will pass on what I believe has worked.

My particular concern is to reach choreographers. When they are ready to stand back and see what they are making they need strategies with which to do so. The mature choreographer has his own strategies. Making dances is a difficult thing to do and some people get hung up on so much inside knowledge about their own work that they cannot find the freshness of an outside eye. I hope to be able to offer some ways which have already done duty in my opportunities to act as a sounding board for makers and their performers.

My second concern is to reach dancers. When it comes to dancing a dance they need strategies too so that they have a range of choices to deal with the material to be danced. That is difficult too and some dancers get hung up on technical problems or on traditional ways of functioning, possibly on their own agenda, and somehow cannot find the way to get into the movement. I would like to be able to pass on some ways that have worked.

It is always a dilemma for a writer to decide whether or not to use the language of ideas in their original form or to paraphrase them into familiar words for a particular readership and in so doing weaken the impact of concepts that are original. Readers may meet some terms from the perspectives of communication studies that are unfamiliar and perhaps daunting at first sight. Several of these terms are in the opening section of the book which lays out the central concepts on how one might look at a dance. The reader may not wish to start here. It is a valid choice to start by reading **The Movement Perspective** if that is a more familiar field of study. The reader could come back to the opening section **Communicating Through Dance** and move on the discussion of the dancer's responsibility in

**The Performer's Perspective** and the way choreographers use sounds and spaces in two further sections. The **Conclusion** looks at several dance works using the notions of communication and semiotics which inform the whole book.

The particular framework used to aid discussion is, to an extent, eclectic because it arises out of dance practice which, as we all know, is ever shifting into new and unpredictable waters. Indeed it is the very fact of the rapidity of the shifts in the content and form of dances created by current choreographers that makes it essential to keep a choreographic eye open to surprise and theoretical issues alive and open to debate.

Included are theories that have proved of interest and value to practical people. What those are is not predictable either for some dance people are rooted in body theories others in semiotics, others in politics or aesthetics, others in history and morphology and others in their own technique. In this book only those theoretical concerns that serve a purpose in a practical situation are included.

Examples to illustrate the discussions were seen as essential. This posed a huge problem for the ideal of having a video with all the examples was just not possible, copyright and royalties being what they are. Nevertheless works are cited and every effort has been made to refer to those that the reader might have seen or have access to.

The best way I can get my word processor to aid me is in format and in type. The book is presented as closely as possible to how we speak to each other. How we normally encounter theoretical things is so far removed from dance that some people never want to look further than the first page of hefty paragraphs. You cannot work in the studio with a page full of theory in your head but you can have one idea, or two, and make them work for your body, your mind and your eye. Hence the break up of the text into many small chapters and short lines.

# communicating
## through dance

# the dance medium : a nexus
## what is the dance medium ?
## what are dances made of ?

Dance people differ in what they regard as
the dance medium.

A medium is the stuff that an art object is made in.
In sculpture it can be almost any three dimensional material
from bronze to wood to plaster to marble to dustbin metal.
In painting it can be watercolour, gouache, oil, ink
or whatever is capable of making coloured marks on a backing.
For to-day's dance what is it ?

All agree that movement is an essential part of the medium.          **movement**
All agree that there must be other elements
in a dance performance,
dancers for a start.
But are dancers part of the medium ?
Are they simply performers of the dance
or are they
an ingredient of the medium out of which the dance is made ?

History tells us, broadly,
that dances and music used to be inextricable,
that this century pioneers took issue with that assumption.
Musicless dances were made.
Movement was presented as the sole medium of dance.
As Mary Wigman put it
"Dance is an art independent of music."

All choreographers have their own views.
Some make their movement with the intention
that it be regarded as the text of their work
that it should be notated,
that the score shall hold "the dance".
In so doing they tacitly state :
movement is the medium of dance
and dancers are the instrument
through which it will be seen.

**performers**

Reconstructors question that assertion.
How the dance material is danced is a crucial concern.
Can any dancer dance the work ?
Are they not more than a body, more than an instrument ?
Can a Graham work be danced by a Bournonville dancer ?
Can a 1990's dancer find the style of a 1930's work ?
Dance directors have argued that
the style of the dance and the style of its dancers are distinct.
Both are essential ingredients to the identity of the work.

How they mesh or miss is the issue
for the personal style of the dancer
together with the choreographic style of the work
makes the performance what it is.

Other choreographers search for movement with their dancers.
Together they discover,
the one dependent on the other.
The dancer's body, personality, creativity, look, gender,
technique, biography
are an essential element
through which the idea is realised.

For some there can be no change of cast.
The dancers who made the work
are inextricable from the work.

**sound**

Music used to come first, always.
It still does for some.
It is essential for most ballets.
It is, with movement, the ballet's medium.

It can be asked of any work :
Was the sound the inspiration for the movement ?
Is it the accompaniment to the movement ?
Are sound and movement integrated, independent,
counterpointed ?
A web between the two is inevitable.
The nature of the web,

the kind of kinetic-aural link,
is as significant as the sound itself.

It is the web, the nexus,
that is essential to the work's identity.
Form is the surface of the work.
Form is what you see and hear.
The nexus is the invisible network of connections
that hold it together.
It represents countless artistic decisions
that arise from the artists' outlook on the world in general
and their outlook on the place of dance within it.

Space is another strand of the dance medium,                    **space**
making four with movement, performer and sound.
"The stage" used to be the assumed space for dance as theatre.
It still is.
So are the field, the video space, the dance floor, the studio,
the loft.
Any space designated as a permanent or one-off arena
where dance shall take place,
is the medium to be contended with.

These places, for some choreographers, are simply a context.
It is viable to perform their movement in this space or in that space
and it is still the work.
For them space is not the medium of dance.
But is that so for all choreographers ?

Space is formidable.
It can kill a dance.
It can make a dance.
It smothers, it cramps, it pursuades, it frames.

For some makers a particular kind of space is essential,
a starting point for the work,
inextricable from the work.
The movement arises out of how the space is,
what is in it,
how it is lit.
For some, the designer of the set
is a co-worker from day one.
For video-dance space is unavoidably significant.

The kind of nexus of the space
with the other strands
is an essential decision to be made for each work.
The connections may do much more than context movement.
They may locate the dancers in a place,

integrate the space with the dancers in action
or co-exist with them in time
as separate autonomous parts.

**the nexus of
the four strands**

Gone are the days when movement was made to music,
danced,
then costumed,
put on stage and lit.
Haven't they ?
Or have they ?

The strands of the dance medium
like locks of long hair
plait into one meaningful whole.
The interlock is all.

**the nature of the nexus**

The web of connectedness
between performer, movement, sound and space
comes in several kinds.

**integration**

Choreographers may choose
to make all elements work together
to support and underpin each other.
Take Martha Graham's **Appalachian Spring** -
Her dancers are characters treated archetypally,
the newly married couple, the preacher, et al.
The costuming underpins the characters.
It tells us who they are and when they are envisaged in time.
The music of Aaron Copland supports the drama.
It matches the tempo of the dancing and the structure of
the scenes.
The set and lighting indicate the homestead,
the domestic scene, the wide open spaces and the
preacher's pulpit.

The style of the work is given
through a gestalt of integrated elements,
none of them totally denotive
but abstracted, suggested,
to create the modern dance drama style of Graham's time.

**gestalt**

Elements given in the performer, movement, sound and space
group together in a gestalt.
Each element is not meaningful,
together they are.
A gestalt adds up to more than the sum of its elements.
Their nexus creates meaning.

When several elements, within a strand or across strands,
say the same thing
the message is strengthened
to a point of redundancy.
Take a lunge forward with a reach forward,
with a lean forward and a focus forward.
Each element reiterates the other.
Are they all necessary ?
The choreographer has to decide on the redundancy of any
elements.

**redundancy and
reiteration**

If his statement is to be obvious
then reiteration is a useful device.
Reiteration, or communicating the same thing again,
by the same means or other means,
serves to give the spectator a second chance to see it and hear it.
In that case it is not redundant
but a useful underlining of the idea.
If the choreographer wants to suggest not depict
then much use of reiteration is not the way.

Putting one element beside another
each of which deliberately conjures an image
with its own context
creates a question mark, a tension.
Do these things belong together ?
    Twyla Tharp started by juxtaposing different movement
    vocabularies.
    Virtuosic ballet is interspersed with mundane behaviour
    in **Push Comes To Shove.**
By doing so she questioned the accepted codes
that ballet is danced by special people, ballet people,
while behaviour belongs to the ordinary person in the street.
The ethereal, elegant and unattainable
was juxtaposed with the earthy and human.
The audience found it hilarious.

**juxtaposing
or intertextuality**

Putting a dance in a contrasting context
is a typical device of Pina Bausch.
    In **Bluebeard** she has dancers in evening dress
    in a space filled with dead leaves.
    The nexus of evening dress and leaf confuses.
    It gives no automatic meaning.
    We have to construct one for ourselves.

**contra-contextual**

Cunningham's nexus is a co-existing one.
Each strand, performers, movement, sound and space,
co-exist in his choreography.
They occupy the same space and time.

**co-existing**

They do not integrate, nor are they deliberately a contrast to
each other.
That is how life is, so that is how art is,
for Cunningham.

The power of the nexus of the strands
appears again and again in the text of this book.
Finding, consolidating and maintaining a nexus
is what the great choreographers have done and are doing.

**reading**

**Walter Sorrell**

Dance in its Time (1981)

Contained in Sorrell's historical perspective are glimpses of the changing
fashions and functions of performers, movement, sound and space in dance
works. It underlines the view that to understand the trends in border crossing in
contemporary performance work it is helpful to locate to-day in the shifting
sand of cultural change.

**Merce Cunningham and Jacqueline Lesschaeve**

The Dancer and the Dance (1991)

Cunningham discusses his works and his collaborations across media. He has his
own way of talking about the strands and their nexus.

**Ana Sanchez-Colberg**

"You can see it like this or like that"

in ~ David Allen and Stephanie Jordan (eds) Parallel Lines: Media Representations
of Dance (1992)

Sanchez-Colberg discusses Bausch's nexus.

**Valerie Preston-Dunlop**

Dance Words (Chapter: The Nexus and Emergence of Style) (1995)

The way dance people discuss the interrelationship of dancer, movement
material, sound and space and how that interrelationship constitutes the style of
choreographers and dance genres is shown through juxtaposing statements from
people working in the field. The compilation gives an insight into the sheer
variety of ways of doing it and thinking about it

# dance as communication
## do dances communicate ?
## how ?

Dance is not a language, is it ?
Or is it ?
Some dance forms communicate directly -
Bharata Natyam for one, classical mime for another.
In those styles each movement is a sign
for something quite specific -
butterfly, lotus, love, marry me, crying.

Some dance forms communicate nothing more than themselves.
They are as near abstract as dance can be.
Yet even they communicate something,
don't they ?

Because ways of presenting dance are so varied
it is not a simple process
to come to grips with how dance communicates.
In this chapter we start from the view :
choreographers communicate their ideas through dance.
In the next we start from the view :
a dance performance does not communicate directly
but contains layers of meaningful elements
created by the various participants in the event
including the spectator.

In reality these two views overlap.
It is just not possible to discuss them both adequately
in the same sentence.

**Jakobson's**
**communication model**

So how does communication work ?
There must be something somebody wants to transmit
and a medium
in which to turn it into a message.
Someone to send it, someone to receive it.
The message has to be put together in the medium
according to rules.
to grammar, to codes, to norms
which other people can de-code,
to comprehend and share.

$\cdot \ \cdot \ \cdot \ \text{—} \ \text{—} \ \text{—} \ \cdot \ \cdot \ \cdot \qquad \cdot \ \cdot \ \cdot \ \text{—} \ \text{—} \ \text{—} \ \cdot \ \cdot \ \cdot$

That is a message,
in the medium of dots and dashes,
according to the morse code
sent by an operative, to convey an urgent need
and received and understood
by those who know the code,
SOS, SOS,
To others it remains marks on paper,
or if heard, just sounds.

**dance communication**

How does dance communicate ?
Somebody,
the choreographer and the co-operating team
have something to say,
or something to share.
Their medium is dance,
that is movement by performers, with sound and in space
into which, with which,
they put their ideas to make a dance message.
Performers then perform the dance message,
spectators receive it, variously.

**codes and conventions**

And the codes ? the grammar ?
There's the rub
for there is no one dance code, no one grammar,
but several.
It is much more complex than the morse code.
Each genre has codes and conventions.
They shift and change as each new style,
even each new dance,
is formulated
and settles its own way of representation.

With no shared code
there can be no communication,
only kinetic / visual / aural non-sense

and sometimes that is just what a semi-formed dance is.

What are dance codes ?
They are inherent in theatre practices.
The audience knows when to sit,
when to stop talking and watch,
without being told.
They respond to an agreed code.
The house lights go down, so stop talking.
The stage lights go up, so observe.
Dancers move about and the music begins.
They stop and the audience claps.

In another culture things happen differently.
Performances last all day,
they occur outside at a designated space.........
only men dance.........
there are no seats, no lights, no stage.........

Movement codes abound too.
Behaviour is one of them.
It is used in everyday life to communicate ideas and feelings,
and to support social order.
It is used in dance both straight and transformed
according to agreed methods (codes),
which we regard as genres and styles.-
expressionistic, post-modern, balletic.

With established codes communication is straightforward.
We know where we are
in Irish folk dance, in Sufi rituals,
in Ashton's ballets, in Graham's dramas.
That is, if we are educated into those codes.
The lack of upper body movement in Irish step dance
we may find odd
or we may admire it in **Riverdance.**
We have to know the code to evaluate the performance
or we can join in which is what it was all about, originally.
In Sufi we may find the endless turning monotonous
or we may appreciate the trance state thereby induced.

We may find Ashton's work old-fashioned
or, if we know the tradition and recognise his unique use of it,
we appreciate his artistry and read his works.
When Graham first came to Europe
she was laughed at by the ballet public.
She had to establish her contraction and flexed feet.
Now we are educated into it,
through it and almost out of it.

So too with post-modern work
with post post-modern work
with Tanztheater
with minimalism, with Butoh.........

Take Carlotta Ikeda's work **Sphynx.**
If you know the codes,
if you can share her metaphors
you will appreciate her profound work.
If not, her way confronts the codes you know.
Her faces are whitened, her dancers' eyes disappear
in their sockets.
Her exaggerated facial expressions may seem ugly grimaces.
Her physicality and eroticism is intense.
Her images and purpose may be unreadable to you
until you begin to get it.
You may have to hear her talk about her work
to unlock the mystery.

With unstable codes
in an emerging avant garde piece, perhaps,
there can be mis-communication.
"I've never seen that before, what did you make of it ?"
With aesthetic codes
there can be mystery.
"It was beautiful but what did it mean ?"
With behaviour codes
there can be narrative.
"I could see they were nervous of something."
And there can be a mixture of codes,
some known ways of doing things with some newly forming
not-quite-there ones,
with some surprises.
And that is how it often is in innovative dance.

**choreographers' choices**

Not all choreographers want to communicate.
Some say they don't mind if they do or they don't.
The problem with that is
as soon as a performance is given,
with an audience,
the expectation of communication is set up.
There is a message, the dance,
even if denied.
There are receivers, the spectators,
even if ignored.
There are senders, even if reluctant.
Codes, aesthetic and theatrical, are set in motion,
something will be given off by the event.
Someone will receive it

as a form of communication.

Spectators are not passive receivers.
They have their own ideas.
They make their own interpretation.
They may see part of the message
or miss it.
They will make whatever sense of it they do,
influenced by
"past experience and present expectations."

There are dances which make it clear
that they are not intended to communicate.
The audience should not receive
but  share.
The dancers should not send
but commune.
The dance is no message
but a ritual, a meditation, a song to be sung together.

**meditative dances**

How the work is framed
clues the spectator into how to look.
How it is made separate from its surroundings
clarifies what kind of art work it is.
By placing spectators in the round, perhaps,
by inviting participation,
the separation of player from audience
so obvious in a procenium theatre
is put in question.

If you want to communicate directly
you have to take these things into account.
If you want to stimulate individual responses
you have to work for that too.
Just to leave it open verges on the irresponsible.

Is communication a must ?
As a notion it is a means
for choreographers to bat against, to question, to ask themselves :
Where do I stand ?
Am I making this for myself
or for someone else ?
What am I communicating ? Something or nothing ?
What grammar am I following ?
What traditions am I embracing ?
What rules am I breaking ?

Have I found a voice of my own, my own grammar ?

**reading**

**John Fiske**

Introduction to Communication Studies (1990)

The communication theories discussed by Fiske, especially those of Jakobson, outline essential features of how we communicate with each other. Jakobson is a linguist. His ideas have to be read cautiously with that in mind for while they are helpful for considering communication in dance they do not address the kinds of issues that we have to address because dances do not all communicate in the ways that verbal language does.

**Pierre Guiraud**

Semiology (1975)

Guiraud expands on Jakobson's work discussing it as semiology, the science of signs and how signs mean. He is also a linguist so the same caution is necessary. He includes discussion on how several signs work together which is helpful in dance since, as a processive art, we communicate over time, one bit of meaning building on what has gone before.

**Susan Leigh Foster**

Reading Dances (1989)

Foster's book is an attempt to look at selected dance presentation modes through semiotics. It is a helpful guide to looking at dances as sign systems written by a dance scholar who is also a practitioner.

# ideas and medium,
# content and form
what is a dance idea ?
is it a narrative or something else ?

The impact of ideas upon the dance medium                                    **ideas**
and
the impact of the dance medium upon ideas
is how dances come about.
It is two-way process -
the fusion of idea with the dance medium,
the giving of form to content as choreographic material.

A vague idea has to become particular.
It has to thicken up,
It has to sharpen, to be honed,
not only in the head but in the medium.

What is choreographic content ?                                      **narrative ideas**
There is no doubt that narrative is.
Romeo's passion for Juliet is content.
Passion is content -
reciprocated and forbidden passion,
young passion.

Is that it ? Is narrative the sole content ?                              **content**

Narrative is the surface layer of content.
Beneath it,
giving it individuality and style,
are deeper layers, all content of a sort.

Lavrovsky's revolutionary attitude to emotion in ballet
in Leningrad in 1940,
with Prokoviev's attitude to Stalinist modernity,
gave a layer of deep content to the Kirov's **Romeo and Juliet**
beyond the story.
Their attitudes to the story,
to the turmoil in the world around them,
to the role of their art at that time
took form as the style in which the work was made.

Tudor's attitude to modernising ballet
in New York in 1943
gave content to his meditation on Romeo and Juliet's tragedy
with the help of the music of Delius.
His way of changing ballet's vocabulary,
of treating music and of handling the group,
became a new content.

In London in 1965
Macmillan's attitude to women's passion
materialised in his Royal Ballet's Juliet
with Lynn Seymour's collaboration.
Such passionate material and dramatic interpretation were new.

Narrative, preferences, emphases, interests,
are all ideas.
Put them in the work's medium and
they become its content.
The philosophy of life of the creative artists,
their attitudes to people, to politics, to religion, to art,
are all potential content.
They become flavours of the choreograhic form.

**plotless ideas**

Take away narrative and what do you have ?
A work with abstract ideas
of bodies, shapes, rhythms, steps, sounds, light.
Is that contentless ?
Or just plotless, without a narrative ?

Attitudes, preferences, emphases, interests, remain
whether there is a story or not.
They become the main content,
together with the fashions and concerns
of the place and the time of creation.

"Form is the visible shape of content"
said Ben Shahn.
The layers of choreographic form are
the kinetic, visible, audible shape of the work's content.

Ashton's **Symphonic Variations**
with César Franck's sound and Fedorovitch's designs
is a plotless classic.
It was made in 1946,
with the Royal Ballet,
the newly re-established establishment company
in London,
a war-weary city longing for peace.
Its content is Ashton's belief in classical tradition,
the relevance of classical order and beauty.

Ulysses Dove's idea for **Vespers,**
a much later work for the Alvin Ailey company,
was not narrative
nor abstract
but about feeling, autobiographical feeling from his childhood.
He recalled sitting in a gospel church
hearing, seeing, feeling prayer,
the energy of the praying people.
His admired grandmother, his own childhood feelings,
the culture of a gospel church,
the trends of the 1980s,
all make his content.

Plotless dance may contain a mission                    **mission content**
to proclaim to the public that
bodies moving is enough,
is art,
that co-existing sound and movement
is as much art as
co-ordinated, integrated narrative.
It was one of Cunningham's aims.

Plotful and plotless dances
may reveal social values -
an appreciation of the ensemble not the étoile,
a reverance for the mundane not the sophisticated,
a detestation of elitism or racial intolerance,
of sexist behaviour, of homophobia.
They are given form in the dance
through choices made,
in casting, in movement material, in group forms.

None of these may be the plot.
They may not be paraded as narrative or as mission,
but be covert in the deeper layers of the work.

Clothing revealing erogenous zones
may reveal a delight in gender.

Unisex costumes question the belief
in dancers as men and women,
suggesting they might be objects dancing.

Muscular physique on women
may give off equality of the sexes
or a particular brand of feminism.
Soloists backed by a corps de ballet
reveal an attitude to heirarchy, to class.
Soloists assembled as equals in an ensemble
suggest an appreciation of democracy.

Movement material, sound material, costume and set design
may be drawn from the everyday.
Unglorified, untinkered,
they reveal a taste for the mundane,
a value for ordinary things.
They proclaim that everyday life
is, can be, aesthetic in its own right.

**embodiment**

The dance medium, the dancers and their moving,
their sound and their space,
are not inert.
They are rarely pure instruments
waiting to take on the choreographer's ideas
unquestioning.

Dances are not made only
by the choreographer's ideas impacting on the dancers.
They impact back.
So does the sound.
So does the space.

Suzanne Farrell inspired George Balanchine through her
physique.
Diane Madden's problem solving facility supported Trisha
Brown.
William Forsythe's Frankfurt dancers co-choreograph.
Almost every choreographer is sparked off by a dancer
or a partnership or a company.

**accidental content**

Content arises from surprising places.........
accidental happenings and unplanned incidents,
the unexpected magic of a partnership,
the physical idiosyncracies of a new dancer,
the near impossibility of some spaces,
the absence of a musician.
All contribute, all can shift the work.

All ideas
act upon everything that happens in the studio.
The choreographer sees what is offered (or doesn't)
listens to what occurs by chance (or not).
He may concentrate on making what he set out to make
or watch as the new thing takes on its own surprising reality.

The embodiment of idea in medium
and of medium in idea
gestates a new object –
the dance, the work, the choreographic theatre piece.
Then it begins to generate its own ideas
and its own style.

**Ben Shahn**

**reading**

The Shape of Content (1957)

Shahn, a painter, addresses the issues of the interrelatedness of form with
content, discussing the content of both narrative and abstract works. He wrote
this approachable book at a time when confusion over the apparent plotlessness
of art works was a current issue. His way of dealing with it serves as a starting
point for the current interest in the communicability of dance.

**Louis Arnaud Reid**

Meaning in the Arts (1969)

Reid's theory of Embodiment in art making, first addressed to visual artists and
to their inanimate art media, is directly relevant to dance where the medium
includes performers who are present throughout the making process and
obviously influencing the processes of creation. Attention to the impact of the
medium on the maker is the crux of his message.

# meaning, signs, in layers
the meanings that choreographers have
during the creative processes,
the signs that are actually in the dance,
the meanings given to it by the spectators –
are they the same thing or three
different layers ?

Go to a dance performance with friends.
Discuss its content afterwards.
It is a common occurrence
that, beyond the obvious, people will disagree.
Ask the choreographer what is in it.
The reply may well be a surprise.

The discrepancy is intriguing.
Whether it matters or not
remains to be explored.
Semiotics is one way of opening the discussion.

Semiotics is the study of signs                                    **semiotics**
and their function in human interaction.
Semiotics of dance is the study of the signs of a dance work.
Signs are elements in the dance
which embody thoughts and feelings in its medium.
Signs, to function, need to be recognisable.
A personal thought / feeling will remain a personal
thought / feeling
unless it is given a sharable form,
one with a chance of being recognised by someone else.

Dances are full of signs.
A forceful gesture on the beat may be a sign.
A gesture, a focus, a light, a pair of shoes are potentially signs.
Put in context in a work
the significance will emerge.

That chair, sat on by that person, in that light
was a sign for 'prisoner' in Christopher Bruce's **Swan Song.**
Some signs are easy to read,
some need to be searched for.

There are several levels of semiotic content, not only one,
to be found in a dance work.
Poietic level signs
arise during the period of making.
Trace level signs are those residing in the actual work,
the product of the making processes.
Esthesic level signs arise out of the imagination of each
spectator.
Each of these three levels adds its own layer.

**poietic signs**

Poietic signs arise from those making processes
which carry meaning.
Anything that influences the ultimate form of the work
is potentially meaningful.

Meaning is complex.
A dance does not have to mean something nameable
to be meaningful.
Many meanings are not verbal.
Feelings are non-verbal.
Recognition per se is meaningful.
It means, "I've seen that before,
I know it, I receive it, I respond to it."

Meaning is both overt and hidden.
It is created by an individual and also culturally derived.
The choreographer makes what he does,
gives the meaning he does,
because he is who he is, uniquely himself.
He lives where he does,
when he does,
amongst whom he does.
He is culturally enmeshed.

An immigrant American choreographer
working in New York
with a background of Russian ballet,
will carry Russia, or New York, probably both,
into his work.
Balanchine did.

Poietic signs are found
in the way the piece is put together,
its structuring method.

They are also found
in the specific references drawn on for the piece,
its images, its narrative.
Both structure and references carry semiotic elements,
for each is recognisable.

For example:
If the work is created out of improvisation by the ensemble
it will look different
than if all movements are created by the choreographer.
The fact of improvisation is embodied in the form,
visible on seeing more than one performance.
The difference is a sign of choreographic method.
Recognising method is part of understanding a work.

If the choreographer were inspired
by the vast spaces of Africa,
its dryness and its rhythms,
those influences may lurk in the work
unstated but traceable.
It is not necessary to make a work about vast spaces
to have vast spaces seep into it.

If the choreographer were moved
by social injustice
or an intimate relationship,
these feelings may creep in to the work,
hidden but traceable.

During the making process some ideas disappear.
They may be purposely abandoned as not working.
They may be thought to be embedded but actually not.
They may be so hidden as to be unrecognisable,
irretrievable by someone else.

What must be present at every performance of the dance,      **signs in the trace**
is the core of the dance, the so-called trace,
irrespective of the differences
that will be overlayed in each performance of it.

The trace is the product of the rehearsal process.
Ideas not in it are lost.
They will not be communicable.
Only what is embedded in the medium
is found in the trace,
both intended and unintended.

Included are those unrecognised ideas
that betray bias, preference,

good taste and bad taste.
They are there, unintentionally,
through choice of costume and music,
through unconsidered omissions.

Here is where a beginner choreographer can be misled.
She may believe that what she intended to put in the trace
is in it, is visible,
when it is not.
Her idea will only be readable if given form in the medium,
in the performer's body, in costume, in movement,
in the sound, in the set.
An immature eye may see more than is there, through hope,
and see less than is there, through lack of experience.

One clear sign in the trace
may be enough
to influence the spectator's eye
for the entire work.
> It does in Galili's duet **When You See God Tell Him.**
> The dancers impact on one another
> in a repeated chest to chest bang.
> The next move of each comes out of the impact.
> His theme that people need to recognise/respond/react to
> each other
> is encapsulated in that movement
> repeated to ensure that we see it.
> From then on only occasional signs are given
> peering out, shooting  a pistol, shaking the other person,
> lying dead.

Identification of the trace
is crucial to anyone remounting a work.
They must know what has to be re-found.
Where there is a dance score,
what that score contains may be regarded as the trace.
It is stable, it is repeatable.
If there is not a score, and there frequently is not,
then the uncertainty doubles.

**signs in the interpretation
of the trace**

What a choreographer has to decide is :
Can the work be danced only by the original dancers ?
Is their input irreplaceable ?
Is interpretational leeway allowable to a second cast ?
Is the original music essential ?
Could the dance be danced without it and still be that dance ?
Can the order of sections change ?
In improvised parts what newness is permissable ?
Are the same venue, the same set, the same costumes essential ?

Can the lighting change ?

Rehearsing a new cast includes work
to ensure that the signs of the trace are present in their
performance.
Choreographers have the right to allow new signs to emerge
when they reconstruct a dance themselves.
Balanchine did, he created a second trace.
It's a matter of choice.

The esthesic level of semiotic content                                    **esthesic signs**
are the signs added into the work by the viewers.
They are imagined meanings
put into it by each viewer, on each viewing,
regardless of whether those meanings tally
with those in the trace or don't.

The response of the spectators to the work
is mostly unpredictable.
The personal mood, expectations and culture of each one
give rise to an individual response.
On first viewing, second viewing, third viewing
the work will never look the same,
not only because of performance differences
but because
the spectator's eye is no longer innocent.
Each viewing influences the next.
As Jauss puts it
"the horizon of expectation" of each spectator
alters as he engages with the work.

The choreographer has to decide
if it matters to him
that meanings will be seen in the work that he did not put into it.
If he wants a message to get across
he has to be sure that the signs in the trace
are strong, are clear, are sharable.
If he enjoys leaving it open, so be it.
It is not a matter of either / or.
Both are possible in the same work.
The artistry lies in saying what you want to say
while allowing the spectator to be touched uniquely
by his own life experience.
That takes maturity.

The four levels of semiotic content in a work are                         **The four semiotic levels**
those present during the making process,
those embedded in the medium,

those added / altered by each performance,
those added by the spectator.

Nijinska's **Les Noces** exemplifies all four.
Here are instances of poietic and trace levels.
The poietic level contains references to the wedding ceremony
of the Russian Orthodox church.
Nijinska did not want to narrate.
She did not want to enact a wedding.
She wanted to embody its elements in the medium
somehow,
so that, if you knew the Russian ritual,
you might get it.
If you did not, you would enjoy the work for other reasons.

The crowns held over the heads of bride and groom in church
never appear as objects.
They are embodied in the supportive group forms of the
friends
surrounding the Bride in scene one,
surrounding the Bridegroom in scene two.

The braiding and cutting of the Bride's hair is a crucial image
of the abrupt loss of virginity in marriage.
It is given in the trace as long ropes attached to her head,
carried by her firends,
ultimately placed round her neck
like a halter.
The braiding is also hidden, as a poietic sign,
in the alternating bourrée of the friends' feet,
in the interlacing of the final group tableau in her home.
If you do not know to look for them
you will see a rhythmically intriguing foot pattern
and an unusual architectural grouping.
They are sufficient to carry your interest in their own right.

Nijinska does put in the trace, with designer Goncharova,
simply and economically,
essential narrative elements.
The parents of the Bride are recognisable
placed side by side, stage left,
with identical arm gestures across the heart.
We read them as a pair in ritual mood.
We are at a home, shown by a small window.

She has to show the parents of the Bridegroom,
at another family home in the same community.
She places them at the side again
but separated, one left one right,

in a house with similar windows
but two
standing in ritual mood with identical arm gesture
except
with a fist not a flat hand.

The trace carries semiotic content
which is expected to be repeatable
but in a reconstruction crucial elements may be missed,
superficial elements may be retained.
Try looking at two remountings of **Les Noces,**
one by the Royal Ballet in London remounted by Nijinska
herself,
one by the Opera Ballet of Paris remounted after her death.
It purports to be the same work
but is it ?
You may prefer one or the other.

Allowing for these four levels is part of choreographic skill
and artistry.
Controlling them is one choice,
ignoring them is another.
There comes a point
when the choreographer changes places with the spectator
to be on the receiving end of the signs,
both hidden and overt.
He searches with open eyes and ears for what is emerging
and what is not.
His essential judgement has to be
what will stimulate the spectator's imagination,
what will drive home a sign that must be received.
"This is what I've done.
Is the idea visible in the work ?
Is it obvious, too obvious, hazy ?"

Choreographers take that experience back to the studio
for the editing processes,
to bulwark the idea,
to underline, to pare down,
to work on interpretation,
to make a stronger opening………

A person acting as a third eye for the choreographer
has to find out what signs were envisaged
in the poietic level,
what the trace and performance contain,
while taking into account that what will be seen
will be an individual esthesic response.

**reading**

### Jean Jacques Nattiez
Music and Discourse (1990)

Nattiez, a musicologist, develops the semiotic ideas of Molino for the analysis of the semiotic levels in musical works, their performance and their reception. The technical terms used in this chapter are Molino's. It is easy to confuse poietic with poetic and esthesic with aesthetic but the meanings are quite distinct. Nattiez's book requires musical knowledge for full appreciation.

### Clement Crisp and Mary Clarke
Making a Ballet (1975)

In the Appendix Clarke and Cridsp show some of Nijinska's thoughts and processes while making **Les Noces.** In so doing they give access to some poietic signs which the viewer of the work might never know about. It is revealing to look at the work a second time having read the Appendix.

### Patrice Pavis
Languages of the Stage: Essays in the Semiology of the Theatre (1993)

Pavis, writing of theatre and literature, approaches the complex topic of reception theory, underlining similar concepts to those of Nattiez and introducing H.R.Jauss's term "the horizon of expectation" of each spectator.

---

# narrative and formal
a look at how the metalinguistic,
the referential and the aesthetic
functions operate in dance works.

If a dance is to communicate
if it is to engage the spectators' imagination
if it is to send them away with a sense of an evening well spent,
then the dances presented
have to contain elements that are worth seeing, hearing, feeling.
"Worth" is a difficult concept
but Jakobson's ideas might help.

Jacobson describes communication                          **metalinguistic function**
as dependent on the codes shared
by the creative artists and the spectators.
Playing with established codes, bending them, flouting them,
is part of a choreographer's stock in trade.
We recognise newness, originality,
because our eye spots the unfamiliar
the new interpretation, the fresh movement,
the originality of the sound track,
the downright subversive.

Jakobson terms this communicative function
the metalinguistic function,
meta - commenting upon
linguistic - the rules of the language used.

He names another function
the referential function.

**referential function**

In most communication the form of the message
what it sounds like
what it looks like
refers to instances, elements, objects, feelings, ideas
that are in the cultural context,
that are in the world shared by both the spectator and artist
and in the private world of each.

Some dances deliberately refer.
They depict, they denote, they narrate.
They tell the audience unequivocably
that something recognisable is going on.
**Swan Lake** does, **Appalachian Spring** does,
**Romeo and Juliet** does.........

Dances rarely narrate with one movement
with only one phrase,
with only one interaction,
with only one leap,
with only one costume.
Because dance is an art taking place over time
at first an idea is only introduced.
On the second, third and fourth time that the idea is referred to
it is reiterated, layered, confirmed, elaborated.

> Take Cunningham's **Beach Birds.**
> Reference one is the title.
> Reference two is the black on white costume.
> Reference three is the arbitrary timing
> which suggests the arbitrary shifts in nesting, sitting,
> roosting birds.
> Reference four is the occasional sharp head movement.
> Reference five is the wing-like sleeve
> hiding the humanness of wrist and fingers.
> The semiotic narrative elements
> are not all presented at once
> as they are in the real life of birds
> but gradually in the processes of the dance's structure.
> No story unfolds.
> No logical narrative is told.
> Gradually the image of birds emerges.

You could say that the referential function is functioning,
processively.

**aesthetic appreciation
and aesthetic content**

In **Beach Birds**
the referential function is pale.
Cunningham is concerned with other things
than referring to birds.

It would not matter if you missed the birdness
for another function is at work,
the aesthetic function.

Aesthetic appreciation
is contemplation of, attending to, dwelling on,
the elements of the dance
for their own sake.
Not because they mean something or amuse,
not because they tell a story,
not because they arouse admiration,
but simply because they ARE.

Aesthetic appreciation is located in a spectator's attitude.
She or he watch aesthetically,
or not.
If not, they might watch for the mistakes
or for the violence
or for the technical brilliance
or for erotic titillation,
none of which are aesthetic appreciation.

Aesthetic content is located in the work itself.
It is how the elements of movement, colour, sound, space,
energy, bodies,
are chosen,
are structured together,
are presented and performed,
so that they are worth looking at for their own sake.
They have to appeal to the human sense of value.

Value
is a difficult concept.
My sense of value and yours may differ.
The parameters of value shift with each generation
but some essentials remain.

For the aesthetic function to function,
the dance needs to be an excellent example of itself
whatever its genre
whatever its type.
The spectator will respond to excellence
even if it is an unfamiliar excellence.

Most formal dances rely on excellence
to make the performance work for an audience.
Each must engender an aesthetic response.
They do it by attending to
the coherence of the elements of the work,

the integrity of the performance of the work,
the consistency of the idea throughout the dance,
the universality of elements of the content,
the quality of the presentation of the programme as a whole.

**the mix in theatre**

The excellence of **Beach Birds**
as an example of a Cunningham work
is never in doubt.
That it also refers to birds is an intriguing bonus.
That it sticks to the code established over decades by
Cunningham
is steadying.

Kristina de Chatel's **Paletta** is a formal work.
Like Cunningham she works within self imposed limitations.
His is co-existence of elements.
Hers is minimalism.
Steve Reich's minimal sound changes,
set at a steady just-faster-than-normal-heart beat pace,
frames and constrains her inventions.

Her motif for four men
is just apparently simple footwork set in an uneven metric
rhythm.
The motif repeats, on and on,
so that pathways gradually emerge.
The motif develops later with strict minimalist methods.

Against the form of the men are three women
moving but in place
each confined within a transparent column.
Their material uses the potential of the column
to support them off the vertical.
Minimalist counterpoint with the men results
in readable complexity.
The theme of black and white contrast
is continued in the costume,
black with minimal white.
The female figures are identical with minimal differences,
primarily given form in individual hair styles,
nothing flowing, nothing flipping,
just varied sculpted heads.

Some choreographers use denotive references
to start a work,
allowing themselves to develop the central idea in sheer dancing.
Suzy Blok slides a cup at Christopher Steel's sugar lump castle
across a dining table.
She knocks it down repeatedly.

He builds it up repeatedly.
Throw a cup, throw you, dance with you.
Swing a chair, swing you, swing with you.
**Still You** goes from the specific to the general.
While the dancing is almost sheer dancing
the music tells us
"I'll kill you, don't fuck up our relationship."
The last image is denotive again.
An embrace and a broken cup.

Gilles Maheu's and Danielle Tardif's **Le Dortoir** is narrative.
The characters are archetypal,
adolescents becoming adults,
given to us through the memory of a middle-aged man.
Expectation is what is set up for the spectator.
References abound in the set,
a derelict interior
with rusted bedsteads on end.
Who lived here ? What went on here ?
It transforms into a pristine convent dormitory
of twelve white beds.
We learn they are for six girls and six boys
their age clued for us through their school-like costume.

After the denotive scene setting
the work proper proceeds formally.
Straight forward invention
on what you can do kinetically with a row of bedsteads,
a metaphor for innocent play.
One step at a time the mode changes, the mood changes.
Trousers off suggests bed-time
and / or emergent sexual awareness.........
pillow fight, pillow play
play / fight, kinetic / erotic
given visually, aurally, motionally.
One step at a time
the action transforms to violence
with place and time denoted
by verbal reference to John Kennedy's assassination.
On through torture and killing, given straight.
An overall message emerges of adult guilt
at the spiritual dereliction of a generation.

**Le Dortoir** uses the metalinguistic function
in its border breaking between theatre and dance.
It uses the referential function
in its depiction and suggestion.
It uses the aesthetic function in its design elements.
The result is a communicative work.

Awareness of the three functions -
the metalinguistic, the referential and the aesthetic
should give choreographers a tool
for the successful engagement of the audience's attention.
It could aid them in their judgement of final editing of their
work for performance.
Am I using the codes of dance theatre ?
Am I refering to the world ?
Am I offering several shades of meaning ?
Is the dance worth attending to for its own sake ?

**reading**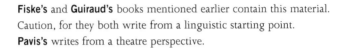

Fiske's and **Guiraud's** books mentioned earlier contain this material.
Caution, for they both write from a linguistic starting point.
**Pavis's** writes from a theatre perspective.

# more on communicating
how do conventions, responses and
interpretation function in dance
performances ?

For the dance to communicate well,                                    **communication**
even allowing for the unpredictable responses of the spectators,
six channels which work together
are proposed by Jakobson.

Given that there are good dance ideas,
given that they are embodied in the medium,
in all four strands of the dance medium,
it is how, and whether, the channels of communication are used
that will determine the success of the work.

Firstly, elements of it are referential.
Secondly, elements are aesthetic.
Thirdly, elements are metalinguistic
as has been discussed.
Additionally,
Fourthly, elements are phatic.
Fifthly, elements are injunctive.
Sixthly, elements are performative.

The phatic element of communication                                   **phatic**
is concerned with setting up the interaction in the first place,
maintaining it
or disrupting it.

In ordinary conversation
we set up interaction variously.
We approach each other,
we look at each other, possibly greet each other.

We keep the conversation going
by maintaining eye contact,
by nodding to encourage the other person to continue,
by remaining near
and by facial expression.

We um and er and add inconsequential sounds
if the conversation lags.
We cut off the exchange
through rituals of dismissal and parting.
Alternatively,
we disrupt the exchange
by inappropriate behaviour.

Phatic elements in dance
serve the same purpose.
We set up the performance / spectator situation.
We maintain it by taking care of transitions,
of continuity, of exits and entrances,
maintaining the illusion and keeping up the magic.
We close it through ritual of bowing and curtains.

Alternatively,
choreographers play with this exchange.
    Lea Anderson does in her highly stylised women's sextet
    **Les Six Belles.**
    She is working with piquant tableaux.
    She wants to play with expectations.
    She does so by blackouts, several of them, shortly spaced,
    during which dancers shift their position, radically.
    A question is half raised : is there a mistake ?
    She retains her communication
    by keeping the sound track solidly in place
    through light, through darkness.
    No, there is not a mistake but a surprise.

    William Forsythe did so
    by playing around with the house lights
    before the performance and as it began
    so that no-one knew when the phatic event was beginning.
    He had the set apparently unfinished,
    backstage crew still at it during the dancing.
    He had a bit of the set fall down, mid-scene.

Such ideas, copied, become gimmicks.
They have to serve a communicative purpose.
They did.
They jolted the spectators into being full-blooded partners
in the communicative act.

The injunctive element of communication
focuses on getting a response from the spectator.
You may want to move them emotionally,
you may want to make them think.
You may want merriment, tears, adulation.
You may want wonder and peaceful absorption.
How you do it is the art.

You could break the rules and shock their sense of propriety.
You could refer denotively to a world event
and set them wondering intellectually.
You could just dance so beautifully
that an awareness of the possibility of human excellence
is evoked.
You could.........

Forsythe broke a phatic rule and got varied responses.
Some people wondered if it were a mistake,
others discussed if they were attending a rehearsal,
some relished the joke,
a few walked out.
At any rate they responded.

The performative element
is the contribution to the comunication added by
the performer.
This, in dance, is such a powerful element
that several chapters are taken to discuss it
under the umbrella concept of intention.
Here all we look at is how the perfomers add a dimension
by who they are,
how they contribute to the other five semiotic functions.

The choreographer can use performers to fulfill functions.
One is cast because of his strength as an aesthetic object.
He is just a beautiful dancer.
He is able to promote the aesthetic function of the work.
One is cast to recount the drama.
She is a persuasive actress.
She refers.
One is cast because he raises issues of ethnicity
hidden in dance codes.
He functions metalinguistically simply by being who he is.
Another is cast because she can identify with the material,
thereby functioning performatively.
Another has a sense of comedy and is naturally injunctive.
These are each functioning
aesthetically, referentially, metalinguistically, performatively,
injunctively.

Dance communicates, doesn't it ?
That is where the discussion began.
Seeing the six semiotic functions in a dance performance
together with the three levels of signs in a performance,
the poietic, in the trace, by the esthesic response,
knowing that the medium is multi-stranded,
give artists a framework
with which to consider their own work.

The choices available are copious,
the pitfalls overwhelming,
the opportunities rivetting.
Coping with that
is what artistic maturity is all about.

**reading**

**Fiske's, Guiraud's, Nattiez's and Pavis's** writings are not put together anywhere else nor are they discussed in relation to dance anywhere else. You can read their ideas separately and then put them together yourself, as I have done in these chapters. Never forget that they are linguists, a musicologist and a theatre theorist, not dance people. The uniqueness of the dance medium with its four strands and its unstable codes requires the reader to question some assumptions in writings on other media and recognise what is relevant and what cannot be.

# performers
## perspective

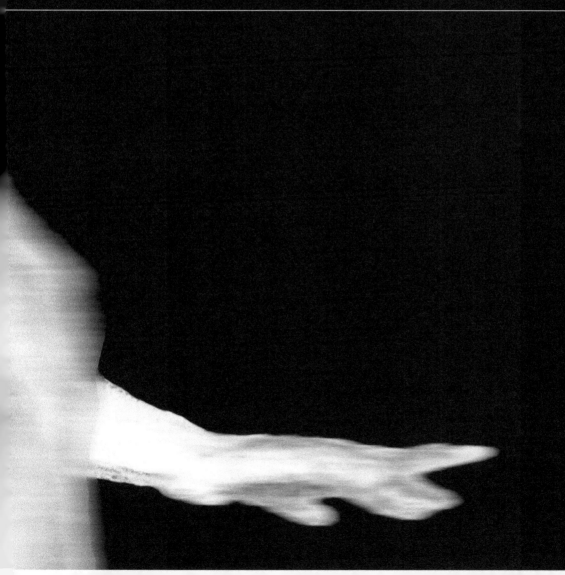

# sensing and intending
how do dancers experience
what they are doing ?

This chapter concentrates on sensing, the next on feeling.
Sensing and feeling are sometimes confused
because words for them
are inadequate and imprecise.
Sensing arises from our sensory channels
our eyes, ears, nose, skin, muscles, and more.
Feelings are different.
They arise out of our response to what happens to us.
They are variants of emotional feelings,
affective feelings and feeling-states,
all of which dancers experience and use.

The body is equipped with senses.                                  **the sensory system**
The nervous system is there to be used
to enable us to experience,
to help us distinguish between different experiences.

When the stimulation is intense                                    **active perceiving**
perception is imposed.
We feel strong pain, we see bright light, we hear loud sounds.
We have no choice.
But
for perception of any finesse
we have a choice.
Experiences have to be sought
by actively searching for the sensation,
by attending to the stimulation offered.

Perceiving is a whole person endeavour,
not a physical one only.
As Martha Graham stated,
art cannot be experienced except by one's entire being.

**attending**

We miss most of the opportunities to experience
because we select what we will attend to.
We cut out swaths of potential sensation
because we have to make sense of a body in an environment
which is bombarded by ambient energy of all sorts-
light, motion, tension, sights, sounds, gravity.

To make use of our opportunities
to perceive our own dancing
we need strategies
to help us attend to what can be felt.

**perceptual channels**

But first, consider the body's equipment.
To sense what we are doing when we dance
we use an amalgamation of information
from inside ourselves and from outside.
To perceive what is outside ourselves,
we have the well known sensory equipment,
visual, aural and tactile,
to look for what can be seen,
to listen for what can be heard,
to feel for what is touching us.

**visual**

Look around.
Had you noticed the colours of the floor ?
the verticals and horizontals of the room ?
the shadows ?
the relative sizes of things ?
the degrees of white and grey ?
Are there greens within your sight ?
Are there hollows and bulges ?

Had you noticed all these things
before you started to attend to them ?
They were there but you chose to cut most of them out
and attend to something else.

**aural**

Shut your eyes and listen to the world around you
and to yourself,
for a minute, or two.
Give yourself time for the layers of sound to emerge…

What did you hear ?
Were you aware of those layers before you attended to them ?
Surely not all of them.

Shut your eyes and feel what your skin                                    **tactile**
and the pressure of the flesh immediately under it
can tell you about your own body -
the soles of your feet on the floor, in your shoe,
your weight on the chair,
the clothes on your back,
your hands, palms, pressure between your fingers,
the pressure of your lips,
your tongue in your mouth,
your breath in your nostrils.
And more.

Were you feeling those sensations before you attended to them ?
They were there.
Until you tell yourself to search, to focus,
you miss so much of what could be perceived
especially of your own movement.

To perceive our selves moving
we have three other channels in addition
that we take for granted.
They are inside information.

The articular system can tell us where the skeleton is,            **articular**
the relationship of one bone to another,
one set of tendons to another.

The muscular system can tell us the tensile state of muscles,      **muscular**
the contracting and releasing of muscular groups.

The vestibular system,                                             **vestibular**
the three semi-circular canals in our inner ears
can tell us our state of equilibrium,
our balance and off-balance states
through the alignment with gravity of our head.

All these channels, the inside and the outside,
combine to support each other,
re-confirming one stimulation by another.
They must, to function adequately.
The visual supports the vestibular
without our knowing it.
Shut your eyes, take a step... your balance is uncertain.
Open your eyes and you can assemble yourself.

Hearing informs us
of the evenness or unevenness of our walking
through the sound of steps,
confirming the muscular control of the body as a whole
and the tactile messages from the soles of the feet.

The muscular
tells us, amongst other things, of our dynamics,
confirmed by the ears
through the sounds of breath, of footfall.

Without this co-operation and confirmation
perception of movement
and control of it
is in jeopardy.
Working together they constitute the equipment
for knowing what you are doing,
for kinaesthetic awareness.

**kinaesthetic awareness**    Dancing feels different,
and looks different,
as we operate each channel of perception.
Dance a sequence of movements,
with your visual perception actively attending to what you do,
to where you are,
to the partial vision of your own moving body.

Dance it again
with the aural channel attending,
listening for your own footfall and your own breath
as well as to the sounds of the room.

Dance it
with the tactile channel attending
feeling your feet, your weight bearing,
the air on your face, the swish of your hair,
the clothes on your body.

Dance it
with the articular channel active
with awareness of the placement of your bones,
the angle of their joints,
now with the muscular channel functioning
feeling the tensing and releasing of your legs,
of your back,
even of your eyelids.

Now dance it attending to the vestibular channel,
sensing your shifts from balanced to off-balance.

How you use perception alters your experience
radically,
and the look of your movement.
Knowing you can use perception
gives you power
over your own performance.

**perceptual power**

You may have perceptual habits.
Do you forget to listen ?
Do you really listen, did you really hear ?
Did you hear what was on offer ?
Do you look at the form of the space around you
and align yourself with it
with finesse ?

Channels have a limited capacity.
You can't feel, see, hear new dance material all at once.
Try it. It can't be done.
You have to take time to get it sorted.
Yoy have to have all your perceptual powers alerted
so that you can
attend to the phrasing of the music,
to the timing of the movement,
to the placement of other dancers around you,
to the dynamics of your own step,
to the amount of turn of your head.
It all happens at the same time.

**perceptual limitations**

Kinaesthetic awareness
has to be a matter of strategies
to overcome the limitations of our sensory equipment.
There have to be choices
so that we can perceive with finesse
the elements of what we have to accomplish.

**perceptual strategies**

Each style of dance requires its own strategies.
Why ?
To perceive its own bodily organisation,
its technical priorities,
its own stylistic embodiment.
A dancer brought up exclusively in one style
learns not only one way to dance
but also one way to feel.

A dancer wedded to the mirror is encouraged to think -
what do I look like ?
What am I feeling may be ignored.
Dancers who use the mirror indescriminately
deny themselves the opportunity to develop

essential skills and habits
of attending
to their own kinaesthetic wealth.

Strategies are provided by some choreographers,
idiosyncratic strategies
arising from the feel of their own work.
Others leave the dancers to their own devices
to connect what they see being demonstrated
with how they feel doing the movement.

Dancers, to cope with all that,
have to possess sensory dexterity,
an openness to different experiences,
a habit of actively perceiving.

We use imagery
to get over the problem
that our channels function inadequately
unless co-ordinated.
Without an overall image to guide our perceptual search
we cannot always sort out
the myriad of sensations available to the body.

For visual perceiving
our language betrays an understanding of the variety of modes
of looking.
We scan, we study, we glance, we trawl,
we focus on, we glimpse,
we inspect, take stock of, observe, regard.

For kinaesthetic perception
there exists no comparable range of words,
only sense, feel, appreciate, be aware of.
But the dancer has to use a variety,
unnamed as they are.

Primarily we can hone in
on one sensation-
the placement of the shoulders perhaps,
the tilt of the head,
the depth and intensity of the focus,
the change of timing in a turn.
Secondarily we can get a sense of a whole
by distancing ourselves from individual sensations,
concentrating on an image that connects them.
Michael Polanyi cites these two ways of sensing
as focal and subsidiary.

We learn new movement
by shifting from one to the other and back again.

Once you can perceive focally,
and get a sense of the whole subsidiarally,
once you are kinaesthetically attending,
once you use images,
then
you can intend, in variety.

Learning to perceive precedes learning to intend                    **intending**
for both are active processes.
In the first the dancer learns to recognise possible content.
In the second
the dancer gives the movement its intended content.

But intention requires a discussion of its own.

**Alwin Nikolais**                                                  **reading**
"Basic Dance and Sensory Perception"
in Dance Observer (Jan 1964)

Nikolais, the pioneering multi-media choreographer, was one of the first to
focus on the dancer's experience. This is a classic article of his on kinaesthetic
awareness.

**J.J.Gibson**
The Senses Considered as Perceptual Systems (1966)

Gibson's writing is chosen from the copious writings on perception as the most
appropriate for dance. He uses the term "the haptic system" for bodily
experience where we might use kinaesthetic. He is one of the few writers
whose work arises from research on people functioning in a normal
environment rather than controlled laboratory research. His emphasis on active
perception contrasts with work in the behaviourist school which emphasises
passive response to stimuli which gives an incomplete picture for how we
function in a creative intending performing art.

Some specialist approaches to kinaesthetic awareness can be found under the
following: Alexander Technique, Bartenieff Fundamentals, Todd Method,
Sweigard Ideokinesis, Moshe Feldenkreis, Laban Movement Analysis, Susan
Klein, Joseph Pilates.

# feeling and intending
## are dance feelings the same as emotional feelings ?

Feelings give rise to movement.
Movement gives rise to feelings.
This in-out and out-in duality,
is the daily experience of dancers.

What are feelings ?                                          **sentiment**
Feeling is a living process becoming aware of itself.
Feelings are overlapping states of varying degrees
with no hard edges between one feeling and another.
They mix and merge in the stream of consciousness.
In behaviour we give them the name "emotion" or
"sentiment".
We try to separate the stream into discrete units -
love, jealousy, sorrow, revenge, awe, amusement.
In reality they are inseparable.

We discern different kinds of feelings.                      **hedonic feelings**
Hedonic feelings
are of liking or disliking something in the world,
our own movement perhaps,
the choreographer we are working with,
a technique style,
a teacher's methods.

The basic 'like'
fractures into love, awe, amusement.
The basic 'dislike'
becomes revenge, jealousy, sorrow.
Some feelings are mixtures of both -
grief, for example.

None of these are artistic feelings.
They are everyday emotions
not feelings that occur through engagement in an art,
through engagement in making a dance
or in dancing it.

**feeling-states**

Feeling-state is a technical term for feeling in the arts.
Feeling-states have very little to do with everyday emotions.
They are those feelings that arise
through the complete absorption
of artists in their medium,
a specific experience of total immersion.
Their aesthetic preoccupation with what is emerging
when idea and medium interact and formulate
gives rise to and arises from feeling-states.
The normal propensity to feel sadness, loneliness, exuberance, merriment
is in suspension.

Choreographers experience feeling-states
as they work in the studio
with committed dancers.
While the absorption in art making is there
it is the feeling-states that arise out of creating in the medium
that are felt.
Slip out of it and you re-enter the mundane.
Disappointment, frustration,
exuberance and merriment return.

Dancers experience feeling-states strongly
through absorption in the movement they are making.
They are no less creative artists than choreographers.
They need aesthetic preoccupation
with the impact of the movement on themselves
and the impact of themselves on the movement.
They have to allow feeling-states to arise.
They will only allow them to
by becoming preoccupied with the movement's form
and its content.

Slip out of a feeling-state into the mundane.
You become aware of your desire for a rest,
your jealousy of another dancer,
your anxiety to please,
your frustration with your technique.
The dance will be lost.

Inexperienced dancers can mistake hedonic feelings
for aesthetic feeling-states.

They indulge in the enjoyment of dancing.
They imbue movement with virtual emotions.
They can wallow in all manner of self deceiving feelings
because they have not yet developed an aesthetic attitude.

An aesthetic attitude is essentially non-hedonic.
It arises from a desire to appreciate the qualities of a thing
for its own sake.
Liking and disliking are irrelevant.
They disrupt aesthetic experience.

In dancing with an aesthetic attitude
you focus on the attributes of the thing you are making,
on the form and rhythm of the movement you are creating,
on the relationships in space and time that your movement
gives rise to
through giving it its intended content and form.
Feelings will arise.
Aesthetic feeling-state will absorb you
as you and the dance you are making become one.

Dramatic feelings are required by some choreographers.            **dramatic feeling**
Imagined emotions, imagined states of mind.
This is how it is
in Rudi van Dantzig's **Monument for a Dead Youth**
first choreographed in the early 1960s.
He required intense feelings to reach the balcony
of a large theatre.
His method is traditional in classical companies.
Dramatic imagination is over laid onto choreographed steps
as the prime device.
His Youth is required to convey
longing, pain, bewilderment, anxiety, guilt, reluctance, passion,
on some occasions while standing still, observing.
Emotions were choreographed by van Dantzig
as archetypal gestures,
as facial expressions, an expressionist mode.
The dancer has to imagine the emotion
and transmit it through the focus and face and enlarged gesture.

In most contemporary work
emotions have to become feeling-states,
a development on expressionism.
They have to be given form in movement,
form which is dynamic and spatial.
The intention is then felt, diffused into the entire body and
lived.

William Forsythe's **Love Songs**
requires the dancer to feel intensely, frantically,
as a person distraught by an ended relationship.
Unlike van Dantzig
he choreographs intense, frantic, distraught movement,
not relying for the expression of feeling on acting
but transforming the feeling into dynamic and spatial form
for the whole body.
The dancers are required to feel
rather than to pretend.

Taking on a role
requires absorption in the character
as well as in the character's movement.
You have to become a persona.
You give up your own person,
your own emotions, to become the other.
Of course it is virtual becoming.
By pre-occupying yourself with the persona's pre-occupations
you can feel as one, one virtual entity.

If you are to become a named character
Medea perhaps, or Romeo,
you have a biography to go on,
a character that you can gradually thicken up.
If you become a more abstract character,
The Red Girl perhaps or A Soldier,
then the movement you have to do
will guide you, will inform you,
will give rise to Red Girl feeling-states,
to soldierly feeling-states.

Awareness of the range of feelings in dancing
the level of passion available and required,
from intense to delicate,
from dramatic to kinetic,
is a requirement for all performers.
Only then can dancers communicate
by giving the movement its intended feeling-state.

Communication relies on the dancers' commitment
for without it the dance remains people moving about.
The dance never emerges.

**Leslie Perry**

"Education in the Arts"

in ~ Dick Field and John Newick's The Study of Education and Art (1973)

Perry, himself a painter and educator, explains the nature of feeling-states in art making as part of an essay on the wider topic of the educational value of art making.

**Louis Arnaud Reid**

Ways of Understanding and Education (1986)

Reid explains feeling in a book whose main purpose is to promote the feeling side of schooling. His first chapters are relevant for our purposes here.

# the phenomenal experience of dancing
# the 'here and now'

## what is phenomenal about dancing ?
## what is the **now** ?

Becoming one with the danced material is what a dancer has to do.
It's not easy for everyone to make the leap
from doing movements to dancing the dance.
If you separate what is done from who is doing it
you lose the dance
because you are the dance.
That is what a dancer has to understand.

Phenomenology offers one view of this leap                     **phenomenology**
by looking at dancing as a so-called pre-reflective experience
as a "not-able-to-think-about-it-separate-from-doing-it"
experience.

It is well known that mind and body can polarise.
We can sit still and think.
We can get up and move with our thoughts elsewhere.
The mind can seem to dominate,
the body can seem to function without it.
In dancing everything comes together.
Laban advised dance people:
"Don't think in words, they separate.
Think through the processes of moving, which is unified."

Dancing is feeling-thinking-sensing-doing
with imagination.
When these get together, the experience is phenomenal.
That's IT.
You have to feel fully and exclusively responsive
to what is taking place, here and now.

Try this movement:  lift up / open out / with energy
You can do it or you can live it.
You can stand outside yourself,
separate your conciousness and your body
and reflect:  am I doing it right ?  do I look good ?
what am I doing ?
or
you can live the here and now of lifting and opening.

**phenomenal time**

Time is experienced, time is organised.
It is both phenomenal and treated objectively.
Stand outside yourself and organise your time.
Look at your watch, go by the clock.
Think in counts, three four, one-and-a-two, seven eight.
Alternatively,
stand inside yourself and experience the now, the present.

Make a simple movement that starts somewhere and ends
somewhere.
Be totally aware of being in the action as it evolves,
every milli-second of it.
Now dance it moving towards the anticipated end position.
Now dance it moving away from the remembered starting position.
You have to dance all three to realise the difference.

Dancing phenomenally is a constant becoming,
not I was, not I will be,
not I was there, not I will be there
but I am here.

We learn dance material by rehearsing
until we get it in the present, here and now.
We watch it demonstrated, we try to remember it.
We anticipate how we will do it move by move
until we have it.
The remembering fades, the anticipating diminishes,
the NOW strengthens.
At that point you begin to dance it, really dance it.

**phenomenal spatiality**

Space is experienced, space is organised.
You can tell yourself to move objectively in space,
one metre in front, quarter turn,
or you can experience yourself advancing and turning

Stand inside yourself and experience space existentially,
as hereness and thereness,
as my space and not-my space,
integrating the "here" motion with changes in the "there".

For dancers
space is not merely occupied physically
but positively inhabited.

Why bother with phenomenal experience ?    **empowerment**
Because it empowers the dancer.
A phenomenal dancer is never an object moving to commands.
A phenomenal dancer lives every movement.
A phenomenal dancer creates every movement
for he turns an instruction into a creation.
If you live where you are
it will take you into the next.

You don't have to be told where to put your body.
You function by becoming,
by stepping, turning, falling, balancing,
by holding still, resolving, dissolving, crystallising.
You solve the problems,
you find the transitions
because you live into them and out of them.


**Fraleigh, Sondra**    **reading**
Dance and the Lived Body / A Descriptive Aesthetics (1987)

**Sheets-Johnstone, Maxine**
The Phenomenology of Dance (2nd. Ed) (1979)

Sheets-Johnstone published the first significant book on dance and
phenomenology. Her opening chapters contain definitions and introduce new
terminology. Fraleigh follows in her footsteps. Again it is her opening chapter
that is particularly useful here for her perspective on the performer. Both books
go on beyond performance into the appreciation of dances which is not relevant
to the focus of this part of this book.

# the dancer's intention
what can dancers do with the
movement they have to dance ?
a look at the dancer's perspective on
the performative function in a work

How does a dancer intend ?
What can be intended ?

In the first place you have to be in the material,
whatever it is, whether you like it or not.
Without intention the dancer is just not there.
"There's no-one at home."
It is like an empty house
waiting to be lived in.

Every dance has roles, dramatic and abstract,
whether in a solo or as part of the ensemble.
The role is the persona you have to become
leaving behind the person you actually are.

Jakobson makes it clear                              **perfomative function**
that the performer of the message
has a strong function in the communicative interchange.
At the bottom line
the spectator will pick up sincerity or insincerity,
identification and absorption
or a tossed off performance.
The art is to be 90% completely in the role
with just enough control to stop you
banging into the wings
or missing the flight of steps.

Every choreographer knows
that performers have the power to wreck the work
or to enhance it.
The performative function is the layer you add.
It has to mesh with the references.
It has to tally with the idea.
You are not a free agent.

Interpreting the role your way
not the choreographer's way
will skew the work's balance.

A beginner can weaken the work
by indulging in feeling
expressed only in the face and felt only in the heart,
in place of feeling devolved throughout the body.
Feeling-states in the posture, in the stance, in the focus
are very different to pretend-emotion.

**commitment**

Choreographers want particular things from their casts.
Energy is one.
Commitment to the high or low energy requirement
is essential,
even if it means sweat, pounding heart, gasping breath,
or holding back with profound delicacy.
Daring is one.
You may be asked to do things you have never done before,
things requiring emotional exposure,
physically dangerous material,
crudity, nudity.
Elegance and poise may be required in a period work,
intense concentration and sustainment in a Butoh work,
grotesque tom-foolery,
long spans of stillness.
All need dancers to commit themselves utterly, appropriately,
in order to colour their material with the necessary artistic
intention.

The Joffrey Ballet's dancers had to commit body and soul
in William Forsythe's **Love Songs.**
It is a suite of dances on the break up of relationships.
"When love goes bad it stinks", was Forsythe's starting point.
Taking Dionne Warwick's and Aretha Franklin's old songs
as a frame
Forsythe exlores the bad, violently.
Sheer daring is required,
reaching for the limit of movement possibilities,
limits of emotional content,
of "out-of-my-mind-ness",

of off-balance danger,
of falls, slides, drags,
with whipping, thrusting, impotent rage.

The persona you have to become may be a character.                **characterisation**
Here we use two well tried roles as examples,
two personalities with a name and a history,
the king Oedipus and the hedgehog Mrs Tiggiewinkle.

The way in may be through research
into who, why, when and what.
You may need to discover the raison d'etre of Oedipus,
how he fits into the plot,
with whom or with what idea he creates a tension,
how his character develops,
when he should dominate a scene or stay in the background.

The approach to the Oedipus tragedy
that each choreographer takes
creates one particular Oedipus, not any Oedipus.

You may need to imagine,
to think the thoughts of this particular Oedipus,
identify with this doomed king,
feel what it might be like to discover your innocent guilt.
Your wife is your mother.
You have murdered your father.
You become the self-condemned outcast.

Mrs Tiggiewinkle is given a definite look in
Ashton's **Tales of Beatrix Potter.**
provided by padding, costume, a wig and a mask,
taken from a famously illustrated children's book.
She is a kindly washerwoman.
Her text gives the clues to her persona.
Is she to be a fussy washerwoman
or an organised person ?
Is she a slapdash washer ?
or a meticulous ironer ?
Is she a forgetful animal ?
or all five ?

Answers to these questions
may help you let your imagination fly.
From there you can find the right feeling-states
through enbodying the images in the form.

In both Oedipus and Mrs Tiggiewinkle
the steps are given.

How you dance them will make all the difference.
In the first place every dancer has to manage the technique.
How to accomodate what has to be done
to their unique facility is essential.
In any season there may be six Mrs Tiggiewinkles,
six doomed kings.
Each one has to find out how best to cope.

A dramatic sense has to emerge.
With a character role it is that
which will develop the sense for tension, climax, resolution,
pathos.

Oedipus is more than a feeling person.
He is archetypal doomed kingliness.
Mrs Tiggiewinkle is all that is magical in childhood.
These things performers and the people who work with them
have to find together.

The dancer and the rehearsal director,
usually work together in an intense and intimate partnership.
Getting out the level of passion,
entering the virtual landscape of the work
can make a dancer vulnerable.
You have to dare emotionally.
You have to allow yourself to feel exposed.
Then you can find the texture of the form.

**questions and images**

Some dancers ask themselves questions
of a sort that might influence movement.
What kind of breathing might Oedipus breathe -
deep, shallow, in the chest, from the groin ?
Where is Oedipus ? In a confined space,
or in a wide open place ? What space ?
Will he dominate the whole scene ?
What level of energy does his persona require ?
Are his eyes looking out or looking in ?
Why does he walk stiffly, why does he turn slowly ?

Imagination is one way of going at it.
Using knowledge of movement,
using the sensory experience of moving,
using kinetic feeling
is another.
In dramatic roles the kinetic way serves the imagination.
It helps find the formal articulation that the dramatic meaning
requires.

For Brumachon's **Naufragés** on Transitions Dance Company
the performers have to imagine and commit themselves
to an array of images of disintegration.
It is a unison work, with no room for individuality.
They have to imagine the horrors of drowning,
and the rigour of 18th century decorum,
so combining the agonised postures of death
with the stylised gestures of the French court.
They have to commit their knees to Brumachon's thumping falls,
their high energy to his spasmic rhythms,
their articulation to exactly what Brumachon envisaged.

How can a dancer interpret formal material ?                                    **formal intention**
It has no narrative.
How does a performer of it function ?
You have to discover the spirit of what your choreographer wants
by working on the material so long
that the form reveals its content.
It is your physical confirmation of that revelation
that distinguishes your performance.

The choreographer may say, "just dance it."
Precision and articulation maybe what he wants,
the actions to be done in just such a way
with no additions but with attack.
Then you have to identify with that need
to give value to it.
Hold back your own views on the material.
Do not let a dramatic vision of your own creep in.

The choreographer may give you material in a basic form
and expect you to make something of it,
expect you to dance it again and again
until you imprint on it something of yourself.

The choreographer may say nothing at all,
just demonstrate what he wants.
He may work with you until he sees in you what he wants to see.
Then you have to sensitise your movement memory
to imprint that moment on your muscles and bones,
on your pace and dynamics,
on your focus and shadow moves.
Only you can produce it again as he wants it
and that is what you must be able to do.

You could use your perceptual skills.
It is here that they might work for you
when imagination is out of place.

**kinetic content**

Knowing what movement is made of
enables you to work like a craftsman to refine performance.
There are always options and choices to be made
on what aspect of a movement's wealth should be shared
with spectators.

All the actual kinetic contents of movement are there -
the body's articulation and kind of co-ordination,
the action clusters to be performed,
the kind of rhythm and phrasing of the movement,
the spatial forms in the material,
the relationships that emerge to people, to the space, to the set.
All these are there to be recognised,
to be sensed,
to be intended with differentiation.

Using the four motion factors is one way.
You can intend one rather than another.
Take spatial form -
You can emphasise the form of your movement
its shapes and its directions
by intending them
rather than the presenting the limbs and joints
that are making the form.

If you intend the flow qualities of your material,
the goingness, the fluidity, the freedom,
and the stoppingness, the control, the tightness
you may add a feeling layer.
It will be subtle but there.
The choreographer may like it
or reject it.

You can be aware of the energy changes
in strength, in delicacy and in weightiness.
If you intend them
it is said that a slight layer of physicality
will be added to the material.
Prioritizing timing, hesitations, accelerations, rubatos,
without changing the basic form
will nevertheless offer another colour.

Working with these kinds of subtleties
in formal material
is equivalent to working with imagination
on dramatic material.
Together you find just the performative layer
that will function for the dance.

In improvisation
some choreographers ask dancers to imagine
that their bodies are functioning
in a way that a body cannot function in reality -
feeling an arm disappears,
imagining one breath going on for ever.
The poetic treatment of the body,
taking poetic licence with it,
is one way of finding an idiosyncratic vocabulary.

**kinetic imagination**

Because you are not the only person in the dance
you need to get a sense of the whole
and of your place within it.
As an ensemble dancer
you have to be capable of being one amongst many.
You may have to take the stage and capture the eye
then to merge in a peripheral role.

**foreground and
background**

Here is an opportunity to use all your skills of sensing
to see, hear, feel what is going on.
Listen to the sound and know what you have to do with it,
pick up on the feeling of the work as a whole
beyond the awareness you have for your part.

Learn to empathise with the timing of other dancers,
synchronising with their pace and energy.
Learn to think of we and us
not me and mine.
The total work is what it is all about.

**Valerie Preston-Dunlop**
Dance Words (Chapter : The Performer and the Movement) (1995)

This chapter of DanceWords collates statements about the performer /
movement nexus. It shows the perspectives on interpretation that
choreographers and critics value as well as the many ways that a dancer can
develop a versatile performance ability.

 **reading**

**Miranda Tufnell and Chris Crickmay**
Body Space Image (1988)

Tufnell describes the kinetic and bodily imagination she uses to give intentions
to her own improvisations.

# the performer's look
## does it really matter what a dancer looks like ?

Performers carry features in their person
that profoundly affect the way they are viewed.
The impact that each has on the dance work that they are in
has to be reckoned with.
It is dealt with by casting issues.

The physique of a dancer is institutionalised in ballet circles.
The danseur noble is a tall, well proportioned athlete,
capable of carrying romantic and noble roles,
a perfect partner for a prima ballerina.
The male character dancer, more individual in physique,
more varied in ethnic characteristics,
is capable of acting, of comedy,
as well as of virtuosic technical feats.

**physique and gender**

Women dancers, equally, are classified.
Usually, ballerinas are not too tall,
are long limbed and slender,
strong but not muscular.
The soubrette is smaller, sharper, piquante in style.
The dramatic dancer may be of any physique.
No ballet dancer must have a gram of unuseful flesh on her body.
Some choreographers look for the placement of
the skeleton in space,
others look for the womanly qualities.

In a classic work
the role informs the spectators about their expectations
of the dancer.
Established criteria enable the regular viewer
to critique physique and sexual qualities.
"Isn't she too tall ?"
"She lacks feminine qualities."
These observations may dominate the appreciation of the work
as a whole.

In contemporary dance no such clear divisions appertain.
Each choreographer, each work, has their own singularity,
their own preferred performers.

The gender of a dancer may be crucial or irrelevant.
**Swan Lake** is traditionally a women's ballet.
The Swan is a ballerina.
It was so, until Matthew Bourne suggested otherwise.
All his swans are male.
Maleness is the point of his version of the ballet.
Gender is integral to the message.

Some ensembles are a group of human beings.
Others are eight men and eight women.
The kind of work emanating from each is different.
Some choreographers prefer to work with single gender companies.
The spectators' expectation of a love theme
as soon as the space is occupied by a man and a woman
is inevitable, but tedious to some artists.

Androgeny has had its vogue.
It raises issues.
Does gender matter ?
Is sexual orientation an issue or a non-issue ?
People are people, aren't they ?

Muscularity may be equally valued in male and female performers.
All have to be capable of physical feats
of tumbling, of falling, of lifting.
Crossing the natural affinity between physique and costume
is a choreographic message maker.
A muscular woman in a black tutu
with jogging shoes and wild hair
crosses the norms and raises questions as well as eyebrows.

While thin dancers are the norm,
works are made that celebrate the variety of the human form.
Why should larger people not dance ?
Why is buxomness in a woman dancer problematic ?

Can the mature male not dance ?
Can disabled people dance ?

Works have been made that explore age
as one aspect of a theme.
    In Victoria Marks' **Mothers and Daughters**
    the age range is maturity through teenage
    to toddler, babe-in-arms to babe within.
    The span serves her idea perfectly.

Companies for the older dancer succeed.
Companies for wheel-chair bound dancers tour.
Works for the slower learner are made.
School shows are put on.
Whatever the cast
the idea is paramount.

Clothing carries meaning.                                    **costume and nudity**
It must serve the purpose of the idea.
Balanchine almost abandoned designed costumes
for simple T-shirt and black tights
in order to priviledge the movement.
That is what he wanted the spectator to see,
not the ballerina, not a danseur noble.

    Stephen Petronio wanted to shock in **Middlesex Gorge.**
    That was the idea.
    He did it in part by baring his buttocks
    while covering everything else.

    Nijinska's political pursuasion
    in response to the changes in society
    of the 1917 Russian revolution
    is embedded in her insistence that
    Goncharova change her lavish costume designs
    for earthily simple, daily, peasant wear.
    In **Les Noces**
    no fairy tale glorification of peasant matrimony is tolerated.
    The costume says it, as well as the movement.

Costumes that restrict the body
limit movement and thereby encourage invention.
They are powerful metaphors.
    In **Aï Amor** Ikeda's dancers are encased.
    Their transparent web both inhibits and reveals.
    Later, the nudity exaggerates her use of the erotic.
    She presents her attitude to the body
    while confronting western codes.

Nudity presents a gendered person.
It may simply celebrate the wonder of the human body.
It may give erotic overtones,
or offer comic possibilities or confront sensibilities.
The nexus is all.

Shoes carry messages.
The first barefoot dancers,
the Duncan and Laban dancers,
the Graham, Humphrey and Wigman pioneers,
took their stand in part by their feet.
Return to the earth was a message,
through soul and sole.
Away with the pretence of the blocked ballet slipper.

Costumes go out of date rapidly.
They follow fashions.
A work can be dated by its feet and its hair.
Shoes to-day are more likely to be jazz flats,
or running shoes, or trainers, or black boots.
They serve the same purpose as did the barefoot in its day.
They set out their value system.

Because the divide between art and life
has been questioned and diminished
in post-modern and post post-modern culture,
fashions in street clothes influence dance costumes
more than they once did.
Illusion dances with illusory characters
need illusion-giving costumes.
Ideas that explore life as it is lived,
danced by personas that are contemporary,
wear to-day's daily clothing.
Or almost.

Problematic are the clothes for dance school shows.
Time and again the shiny unitard
in jazzy pink or orange, blue or rust,
costumes a work that attempts a perspective on a serious topic,
albeit at school level.
But what message does the orange nylon unitard offer ?
Certainly no teenage young man would wear one.
The unitard begs the question:
Is dance for girls only ?
The variety of bodily development of the young dancers
is displayed by it.
The flat-chested, the broad hipped, the heavy thighed,
the anorexic girl,
are inevitably exhibited.

Is that what the dance is about ?

Although hair is a small issue, apparently,
it is nevertheless there.
Cloned hairstyling is part of the ballet tradition.
The neat head coiled into a bun
is a metaphor for observance of the rules.

Individuality is expressed in hair styling choices.
Tolerance for alternative perspectives on life in general
is expressed in hair styling.
The long haired man, the close-cropped woman,
the sweeping blonde, the tossed-back brunette,
the shaven head, the pink-dyed mop.........
all carry messages.

Choreographers and designers
pay attention to hair
because it speaks loudly
of the story of the work,
of the politics of the company,
of the value system of the school.

**hair**

Dancers carry in their bodies an acquired technical capacity
according to the styles in which they were trained.
A Limón dancer's use of weight is entrenched.
A Graham dancer's habit of starting the movement through a
pelvic contraction
is visible.
A ballet person's stylised arms, fluidity, stretched feet, will
always be there.
Over and above the learned technical style
is the personal style of each dancer.
It is a mixture of many ingredients
some of bodily origin and some of personality,
some of understanding.
Dancers are known for their uniqueness,
for what they offer the dance beyond good dancing.
The significance for casting
lies in the mesh of personal style with the style of the work.
It does not always happen.

**technique
and personal style**

Ulysses Dove found this when working with the
Royal Swedish Ballet.
**Dancing on the Front Porch of Heaven** is about loss,
losing people, people dying, loss of loved friends.
His work divided into love, friendship, loss, letting your spirit go.
Even with the sound of Arvo Pärt's
**Cantus in Memory of Benjamin Britten**

the Swedish dancers just did not understand.
They turned the work, said Dove, into beautiful sculpture.
Dove created a work about form and feeling.
What was danced was one about form.

The look of a performer is a strong signifier,
stronger than the references in the movement.
The look is a combination of elements
that an experienced choreographer
will deal with, automatically.
What a dancer looks like
influences how the movement performed will be perceived.

**reading**

**J.Gaines and C.Herzog**
Fabrications: Costumes and the Female Body (1990)

**Susan Leigh Foster**
Corporealities: Dance Knowledge, Culture and Power (1996)

Foster edits a collection of essays which focus on the body as meaningful
in dance

**Valerie Preston-Dunlop**
Dance Words (Chapters : The Performer and Costume) (1995)

# movement
## perspective

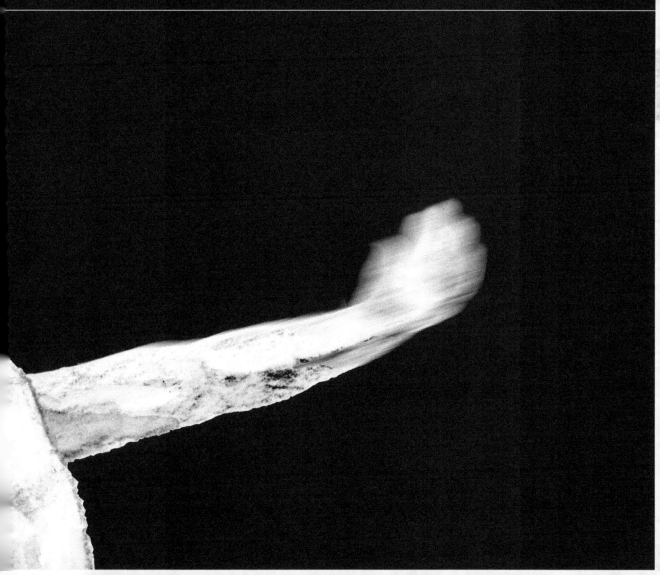

# the factors and vocabularies of movement

what is movement in dance made of ?
what are dance vocabularies ?

Cunningham states the components
of the dance part of a choreographic work
to be movement of dancers in space and time.
He takes a structural view of dance
paring down the form to what he sees as the essentials.

The structural components of movement per se
are the essentials.
They are what must be there for movement to exist
irrespective of its motivation, its references, its intention.
They are seen generally as
bodily coordination of all sorts,
actions in variety,
time and dynamics of the actions,
spatial forms made by the actions,
relationships within the body
and between bodies.

These five are always present in a movement.
You cannot move without them.
Some part of the body acts, bends or twists perhaps.
It does it with some timing and dynamic force.
By doing it a pattern of some sort is made in space.
By doing it the body's limbs change their relationship to each other.

People start with any one of the components
when making movement.

**the components
of movement**

You could be interested in direction and shape.
The directions and shapes have to be made by a body.
In so doing bending, twisting, transfering weight occur.
Inevitably timing and dynamic change.

People start with timing and dynamics.
Others with how bodies touch and support each other.
The components combine in incredible variety.

Each main component consists in several elements.
The following chapters take each of the five
and discuss their possibilities.

**vocabularies**

Here we consider
how the possibilities within the components
are selected to form vocabularies of movement.

Components combine into established vocabularies
according to rules and codes.
Folk dance steps, holds and group patterns are one,
Ballet pas and port de bras make another,
musical comedy and jazz routines,
acrobatic material, T'ai Chi postures,
Graham and Limòn materials,
the sign language of the deaf,
the behaviour of all of us,
children's games and soldiers' drill,
Capoeira, social dance,
and more,
are distinct vocabularies of movement.

**ballet**

The choices within the five movement components
in ballet and behaviour
are compared here
to exemplify the differences in the structural content of vocabularies.

Ballet prioritizes a particular co-ordination of the body.
The legs work independently of the rest of the body
restricting their actions to named steps.
The arms work from the sternum not the solar plexus.
The head has particular tilts and turns
according to the port de bras
and to where the dancer is facing.
The hands and fingers are held in a stylised way,
not stretched or in a fist.
The legs are out-turned not in-turned or parallel.
The feet are extended not contracted or loose.

Ballet chooses certain spatial directions and not others.

It prioritizes verticality above all else.
The basic dimensions of forward and backward, right and left,
are second.
It values peripheral pathways in space for the arms
and avoids central ones.
It contrasts the straight line of an arabesque
with the curved form of an attitude.
It avoids fragmented and broken lines,
spirals and twisted forms.

Rhythmically ballet chooses
the regular metric rhythms of classical music.
It avoids breath rhythms, or free rhythms, or irregular metres.

Ballet dancers work alone,
with imaginary spectators as the people with whom they relate,
out there.
Their duos are predominately for one male with one female
in pas de deux and partner work.

From all the possibilities of each component of movement
ballet has selected those that fulfill its aesthetic.
They create its form, its morphology.
They embody its value system.

By contrast, behaviour prioritizes quite different elements                **behaviour**
according to its rules and codes.
To start with behaviour is motivated by the felt need
to socially interact.
Aesthetic criteria occupy a very small part of its concerns.

The units of behaviour are not fixed as they are in ballet.
They are apparently open,
but organised through tacit parameters
beyond which the behaviour is regarded as odd.

Geometry is not the basis of its spatial organisation
as it is in ballet.
Rather behaving is organised spatially around
towards and away from,
above, beside and below,
opening out and closing in.

Rhythms in behaviour are not metric.
They arise out of the actions being done
and out of the mood and emotional state of the mover.

Relating to other people and objects
is central to behaviour.

We move towards and way from people,
touch people, look at people copiously.

The point is
the same component categories of movement are used
in all movement vocabularies.
The motivation behind each, its value sytem and purpose,
engenders choices.
Hence the variety.

**vocabularies in
choreography**

Choreographers make dances out of movement
in a web of interdependence
with performers, with sound and with a space.
They chose to do so
EITHER
with received movement vocabularies
such as those  cited
or whatever other vocabularies they know.
The interest lies in what they choose
and in how the vocabularies are structured together.
Twyla Tharp has done so,
David Bintley has
and many others.

OR
Choreographers take vocabularies
and alter them,
changing whatever constituents in them
seem pertinent to the overall idea.
The interest lies in the idiosyncratic way
in which each choreographer goes about it.
George Balanchine did so with ballet,
so does Christopher Bruce and Rudi van Dantzig.
Lloyd Newson does so with behaviour,
for example.

OR
Choreographers start from scratch
not using anything received.
They make their own vocabulary
out of the components of movement.
Martha Graham did.
Mary Wigman did.
Alwyn Nikolais did.

In order to alter a vocabulary
or structure several together
or make one anew
you have to work with the components of movement.

Possibly you have to discover new elements
within the categories
so that you can fashion or re-fashion dance material.

Understanding what a vocabulary's parameters are    **altering**
in terms of its structural components
and its rules and values,
can assist in suggesting how a vocabulary might be altered,
be personalised.
That is where most beginner choreographers start.

Altering, to be successful,
has to have a purpose.
By its nature, altering is metalinguistic.
Playing with codes, changing them, flouting them
has an iconoclastic tendancy.
Iconoclasm for the sake of it verges on vandalism.
Change for the sake of change only is unsuccessful.
Iconoclasm in order to break down an irrelevant belief
or an out of date way of expression,
has to contain some idea
as to what will replace the rejected icon.
Master choreographers have a coherent vision
of what that is for them.
Inexperienced choreographers have a problem, understandably.
They start with what they have learnt
and alter it through intuition and emotional feeling.
Intuition and feeling are necessary
but insufficient on their own.

It takes another sort of talent to mix vocabularies successfully.    **mixing**
Mixing is itself a reflection of the wish to break down barriers.
How wide the mixing will be is individual.
      Shobana Jeyasingh mixes Classical Indian dance
      with Purcell music and contemporary dance,
      in **Can They Tell Stories.** Quite a mix.

Twyla Tharp mixed anything and everything
from baton twirling, to tap dancing,
to ballet to behaviour in a successfully eclectic melange.
When she started that was utterly radical.

      Bintley mixes in **Still Life at the Penguin Café**
      within the range of vocabularies of the conservatoire -
      character dance, musical comedy, social dance, ballet.

It takes a radical pioneer of extreme talent and perseverence    **new**
to create an entirely new vocabulary
founded on a personal belief and philosophy of life

and extensive studio work.
Nothing that could be written here
would contribute to such a gift.

Many innovative choreographers
make entirely new movements
combining them with established vocabularies
so making works that are both readable and fascinating
in their newness.
    Kylian offers a prime example in **Kaguyahime.**
    Tuerlings does with **A Noeud Couland !**
    As you watch you can recognise moments and elements
    and then be surprised.
    The mix may draw you in.

What follows in this section of this book
concentrates on movement in detail.
How to look for movement material, how to look at it,
how to set about altering it,
how to put a personal stamp upon it.
What kinds of structuring have been used
to turn movement material into dances
is included.

**reading**

**Marcia Siegel**
The Shapes of Change (1979)

Siegel, writing as a New York critic, focuses on the movement content of works
of the 1960s and 1970s.

**Sally Banes**
Writing Dancing in the Age of Postmodernism (1994)

Banes, a specialist in Postmodern dance, is able to describe dances and their
function.

**Stephanie Jordan**
Striding Out (1992)

Jordan concentrates on British experimental dance, describing its movement and
structural content.

# behaviour as a movement vocabulary
can psychologists' and sociologists'
and movement people's understanding
of behaviour offer the choreographer
a tool ?

Behaviour is one movement vocabulary.
Like any other movement vocabulary for dance
it is observed, collected, used straight, used altered,
is inter-mixed with other vocabularies
by all manner of structuring methods.

Behaviour is also a favourite topic for a work
explored by choreographers
as the substance of both narrative and so-called abstract works.
Copious dances are made of it, with it and about it.
    Take Martha Graham's dramas.
    Take her more formal work **Diversion of Angels.**
    Take Bausch's **Café Müller,** take Vandekeybus and Lloyd Newson.

Michael Argyle, a seminal figure in psychology,
looks at behaviour
as socially motivated social techniques.
He asks the questions :
why do we interact socially ?
how do we interact socially ?
He does not provide all the answers
but some that have proved useful for dance people.

Social techniques are the means we use          **social techniques**
to communicate our social needs and goals.
These include the means used within a culture
to signify non-verbally and verbally.

They carry messages
because we have tacit rules of behaviour
for orderly and disorderly conduct,
for balanced and unbalanced behaviour.
We focus here on the movement means he cites.

**bodily contact**

Bodily contact is the first.
The physical contacts in aggressive behaviour
and in sexual behaviour
are familiar.
Hitting, slapping, kicking,
tripping up, wrestling, pinching,
contrast with
caressing, stroking, hugging,
embracing, kissing, penetrating.
All manner of other contacts are made
each one part of a power game.

Try a tap on the shoulder, a tap on the head,
a pat on the back, a dig in the ribs,
smooth a lapel, straighten a tie,
ruffle the hair or grasp an elbow,
shove your way through a crowd.

Taboos operate for bodily contact.
For heterosexuals strict rules apply
for a man touching a man.
Even more restrictive are the codes
for women touching each other, so Argyle tells us.
Touch the forbidden surfaces
of someone who is not an intimate
and you will get a swift reaction.

The expression of unsuccessful social touch
is shown in many dances,
for isolation and loneliness are common themes -
an embrace with straight arms,
a caress of the cheek with spiked fingers and back of the hand,
a pat on the back that turns into a slap,
a hug that squeezes.
> Gadès in **Blood Wedding** captures the poignancy
> of forbidden love
> through imagined touch, with the partners at a distance.
> Newson in **Strange Fish** captures the hopeless attempts
> at intimate touch
> of the socially inept Nigel.

There is a problem with touching in some contemporary dance
where many bodily contacts are purely formal or functional.

"I turn you, you turn me."
Many derive from contact improvisation,
the democratic duo form of dance
where dancers are essentially co-operative.
They avoid dominance,
they eschew sexual content or aggressive overtones.
They ignore the social taboos of touch.
So the expressive charge of touch
so strong in daily behaviour
is minimised as communication in dances thus derived.
The pair get on well,
no power struggle, no social interest,
no tension to be resolved.
But the spectator may look for them
for where two people occupy each other's space
something is going on...
anger is triggered, love blooms.........
When they do not see it
spectators may switch off.

Proxemics is the study of proximity and position          **physical proximity**
of people while interacting.
The region around each of us,
our personal space,
we treat as if it were a part of our body substance.
If anyone intrudes into that space without approval
we react as though invaded.

We welcome someone into our personal space closely          **intimate and**
as an act of intimacy.                                       **personal distance**
It is a clear signal.
Forced proximity is resisted.
It diminishes individuality.
We cease to be one person, we become a herd,
a crowd.
Get into a rush hour subway
and experience it.
Space speaks.

Social distance, beyond reach distance,          **social distances**
used by colleagues not friends nor enemies nor lovers,
is the nost neutral interpersonal space.
It is the dancer's class distance,
an oft-used choreography distance
to avoid clashes of arms and legs.
The theatrical message of this space is muted.

Public space is even further -
the distance between one side of the stage and the other.

This distance can speak of power, of longing,
of status.

**spatial positioning**

Facing vis-a-vis confronts,
inviting dominance or dependence.
Standing side by side gives off equality.
It makes communication awkward between the two.
Diagonal facing eases interaction
without making it confrontational.
One behind the other ?
Higher than, lower than, above, below, on level with,
all speak of dominance games.
They are more than spacing for its own sake.
They are spacing that communicates human motivation.
Never forget, space speaks.

**gesture and posture**

Gestures, meaningful movements of isolated parts,
postures, meaningful movements of the body as a whole
are copious in behaviour
as conveyors of messages.

Just observe people
anywhere in a public place where interaction might occur.
Observe and collect items of movement,
from top to toe
as material for dances.
Look at the head and neck, closely,
the chin tilt and the hair.
Look at hands, their touch, their gesticulation.
Look at the stance, closely,
on one foot or two, on heels or toes, even or uneven.
Look at the torso, the hips, the chest.
Each has a repertoire of dynamic qualities
through timing, energy, flow, size.
Each move is potential material,
small in size but great in expression.

Ritualised gestures abound
in handshakes, waves, thumbs up, thumbs down,
in shrugging shoulders, clenched fists, nodding heads.
We use them and we know their meaning.

**shadow moves**

But look again at the smaller moves,
the shadow moves,
idiosyncratic ways of doing things.
Look for their dynamic, their timing,
their tension and their counter-tension
for they are pregnant with expressive possibilities.

The relation of posture to gesture
is a crucial signifier.
Gestures on their own, unsupported posturally,
are largely an acquired repertoire of moves
many ritualised or functional.
A gesture supported posturally
with the torso or stance or breath behind it
betrays personal involvement.
Just try greeting a sort of friend
or greeting your love.
Posture / gesture mergers (pgms)
give off truthfulness.
You mean it.

posture / gesture
mergers

> The unity of torso with arm movement
> is a style ingredient of Kurt Jooss's work.
> His was a colossal shift in style from the balletic elegant
> use of the torso
> to the modern realist use of it in the 1930s.
> Ballet companies who mount Jooss's **Green Table**
> have to spend much rehearsal time
> learning an unfamiliar kind of posture / gesture merger.
> Once achieved, it gives off his kind of integrity.

In conversation, in non-verbal exchange
we use our faces to convey our feelings
through muscular changes
in eye, brow, mouth, cheek, nostril, forehead, tongue.
Research tells us
that the eyebrow flash is a universal sign of recognition,
that symmetric and asymmetric frowns tell different stories,
pouting, grinning, smirking, gnashing teeth,
mouth corners up and down, with and without a tilt of the head
all speak, in a context.
Mouths can speak volumes, non-verbally.
Just try it, with someone watching.
Press your lips together, lick them slowly, purse them.
Push them forward a little, a lot,
open your mouth, slightly, drop your jaw,
smile this way, that way, and the other.

facial expression

In some dances, oriental more likely than occidental,
head and facial movements are a denotive language,
highly skillful, highly complex,
describing character and action.
In some current western dance
the face as a whole may be bland
ostensibly saying nothing
actually saying: I'm not a feeling human,

I'm not here, this is just my body.

Grinning at the audience, smiling at them falsely,
attempting to give off gaiety and energetic enjoyment
can still be seen in some dancers and some productions,
encouraged by someone, believed by no-one.

Dexterity in facial expression requires awareness
and rehearsal and honesty.
Tensile conditions in cheek, around eyes, flaccid or taut,
occur naturally with intentions of all kinds,
in minute portions as shadow moves,
discernible but not paraded.
Feel how your face changes as you give movement content.

> Lea Anderson requires this from Transitions Dance Company
> for her highly stylised work for women **Les Six Belles.**
> She carefully collects her facial expressions
> as well as gestures
> from an event or a film or an exhibition.........
> anywhere where deliberate and cohesive expressiveness will
> be evident.
> Eye, eyebrow, nostril are all choreographed
> These minute changes with their dynamic and spatial clarity
> are what the dancers have to perfect.

**focus and eye
movements**

Focus in dance is hugely important
as any choreographer and any dancer knows -
the direction of gaze, to which distance,
with what intent and with what dynamic change,
focused or glazed, directed or averted,
with closed eyes, with lowered lids or wide open.
Try it out as you dance.
Focus gives potent communication
for focus is created by intention
and intention speaks.
Focus is reflected in shadow moves of posture and gesture
and that enhances feeling.

**the non-linguistic
aspects of speech**

Argyle tells us that
not only the sense of the spoken words
but everything in speech, over and above the words themselves,
communicates -
the speed of speech, the stops and starts,
the ums and ahs,
the interruptions, the silences,
the emphases.
Sighing, groaning, tittering, laughing, howling, gasping,
holding of breath,

in fact the whole gamut of emotional sound making
and the expression in sound of interactions,
the whole gamut of their dynamics and phrasing
communicates.

For dance this alerts us
to the potency of speech idioms.
    Some choreographers include them just as they are -
    laughter as material, speaking dancers.
    Pina Bausch did in **Kontakthof.**
    Some translate them from mouth to body,
    tittering in the shoulders and feet.
    Lloyd Newson does in **Strange Fish.**
Some diffuse them in the dynamic qualities of the steps,
while some embed them in the movement's spatial form.
Some exaggerate, others abstract.

All the elements of social techniques cluster in phrases
to convey the complex ambiguities that fill out social exchange.
For the dance person they are a resource.
For choreographers they are potential material
and a potential topic.
For dancers they are a source for interpretation
and material to be learned.
It takes practice
to acquire the technique to perform minute gestures
but some choreographers demand it.
For spectators and critics
they are a lifeline to reading a work,
a kind of dictionary of behaviour.

**social techniques
and dance**

For all, the skill of observing is the clue.
Set yourself to look at people interacting,
to study their bodies, their postures, their stances,
their use of space, their eye contact, tilt of head, thrust of chin.
Collect units of behaviour, of touches,
as an artist collects in a sketch book.
Once your eye is open and your perception in tune,
the world is your oyster, as they say.

**Michael Argyle**

The psychlogy of Interpersonal Behaviour (1967)

This is Argyle's first book which describes comprehensively his findings. He
contributes similar material in many later books on behaviour. This one outlines
social motivation and social techniques.

**reading**

### Edward Hall

The Hidden Dimension (1966)

Hall's work on Proxemics is well known and much quoted. This is the book in which he first presented his research in an approachable text.

### Warren Lamb

Posture and Gesture / An introduction to the Study of Physical Behaviour (1965)

This is Lamb's first text. His later writings apply his findings on physical behaviour to management teams while in this early book he outlines his theory for the general reader.

# bodily co-ordination
## the first of the components of movement

Bodily co-ordination is the way
the limbs and the torso and the head
function together.

If they work congruently
then all the bits of the body work as one.
Nothing is left out of one concerted statement.

The bodily style used in expressionist dance was congruency.
The soul initiated the concerted move,
the centre of the body
being the core of the expression.
Congruency can look dated.
It may also be chosen for emphasis
in a dance otherwise using body fragmentation,
an effective device.

**congruency**

An isolation occurs
when a part moves on its own,
independent of what the rest of the body is doing,
or not doing.
Jazz dance prioritizes isolations
Body fragmentation through clusters of isolations
could be a metaphor for an inner state
of dislocation.

**isolations**

All movement has to originate somewhere in the body.
Guidances, initiation, leading with,
are ways of describing origination.

**central and peripheral
initiation**

A central movement starts somewhere in the middle of the body
and radiates out into the peripheries.
What people regard as "the centre" is crucial to style.
Movement in the Graham style starts low down, in the pelvis.
Every contraction occurs there.
Every release relates to there.
Port de bras in ballet start high up in the sternum.
For Limòn style the centre is the centre of weight.
For Isadora Duncan it was the solar plexus.

Peripherally led movement
starts in any peripheral bit of the body,
in the fingers and toes,
in the top of the head
and remains out there.
Central and peripheral initiation feel and look distinct.
They reflect different points of view
on self presentation.

**sequential and
simultaneous flow**

Flow of energy can pass through the body
in a fluid succession,
from the centre outwards,
from the periphery inwards.
Successional movement happens in the arm,
or only in a hand,
throughout the body in a body wave,
or from the hip through to the foot.

Rather than passing sequentially through adjacent parts of the body
the energy can be co-ordinated simultaneously.
The leg moves as a whole unit,
the wrist and hand work as one piece,
all vertebrae of the spine move together.

**inclusions and
reflections**

Although one part of the body may have the main statement,
how the rest of the body is included or excluded
matters.
What at first sight and at first feel
might seem to be an isolation
is radically altered in its message
if it is reflected in another part of the body.

The main movement might be a stamp
reflected by a sharp juddering of the torso.
It might be a soft sweeping of the arm
in which the shoulder girdle but not the whole torso
is included.
It may be a run backwards

in which absolutely no response in the rest of the body is wanted.
Choice has to be made.

One movement countered by another                              **counter-tension**
is a way of moving with a powerful message.
By pulling away in opposite directions,
by two gestures pushing across each other,
by an arm lifting against a downward head,
unresolved tension is the image given.

Expressively, there exists a special relationship              **postural support**
between gestures and postures.
If a gesture is isolated,
unsupported by the rest of the body
it gives off a radically different message
from the same gesture reinforced
by a reflection in the rest of the being.
However slight that reflection might be
it exudes personal commitment on the part of the mover.
Unsupported gestures
give off constructed meanings, contrived statements.
Both are important message givers.

The differences between forms of bodily co-ordination         **subtlety**
are not always large, simple or obvious.
Subtle movement contains
a main co-ordination with a second one as overtone.
A choreographer may say one thing
while actually demonstrating a second colouring
through a suggested counter-tension,
or a softening of a gesture through sequential flow.

Dextrous dancers learn to watch closely.


**Miranda Tufnell and Chris Crickmay**                         **reading**
Body Space Image (1993)

A way of imaging the possibilities of the body as an expressive improvising
instrument is described here by two practicing dancer/choreographers.
Their approach complements the discussion of bodily co-ordination given in
this chapter.

**Valerie Preston-Dunlop**
Dance Words (Chapter 7 : Movement and the Moving Body) (1995)

Sections on Co-ordination, Isolations and Body Articulation in this chapter
contain collections of statements on the point of view of various dance artists
and writers to the use of the body in movement.

# actions and steps
## the second component of movement

Actions are what the body does.
They occur in the body as a whole
and as isolations
of one limb, of one joint, one bit of you.

Steps or "pas"                                                    **steps**
are created action clusters,
several actions of limbs and torso and weight linked together
to make a recognisable and repeatable movement.

In codified vocabularies
steps have names :
    pas de bourrée in ballet
    break step in tap
    backward fall in Graham
each being a polykinetic movement.
Choreographers name their newly emerging "steps"
"the fish-over" ...... "the third knot" ...... "the bison leap"
to aid memory and communication in rehearsal.

Steps are made up of individual actions,
given particular spatial form,
particular rhythmic form,
particular co-ordination of the body.
In this chapter we are looking at the action only.
Spatial form and rhythm are discussed later.

**actions of the
whole body**

Actions are described here as categories of movements :
    transfering the weight
    travelling
    jumping
    turning
    over-balancing
    holding still.
These are well known actions made by the body as a whole.
They can be stunning when used significantly.

Recognise them in your own work.
Try them out,
not only in the most obvious way.
Find fresh material.
    Take a look at Hans Tuerlings' *A Noeud Couland !*
    His action invention is just that,
      fresh and unexpected.
One way to go about it
is to impose rules of play on yourself.
They might be :
never complete a movement entirely,
allow it to stop in mid air;
go further than you think in a movement,
when is seems to have ended take it beyond the comfortable;
identify the most natural movement to come out of the one you
are doing,
deliberately never do it, do something else.

**transfering the weight**

Transfer by sliding, falling, rolling,
by placing the weight deliberately.
Go from one foot to another
from heels to toes, from seat to knee and palm
to back, to right hip.
Your weight was there,
it is now here.
Feel it.
Intend it.
Just one transfer has a myriad of possibilities.

    Contrast de Chatel's economic minimalist stepping in **Paletta**
    with Forsythe's expressive exploration of transfer variety
    in **Love Songs.**
    Both are memorable.

**travelling / locomotion**

Travel away from where you are
by stepping, by running, crawling, limping, shuffling,
rolling, sliding,
by all manner of improbable ways
that you can find yourself.

Start on your left hip and just go.
Find a way.

Travel to arrive somewhere.
Travel to leave something.
Travel to revel in travelling.

The traditional jumps are :                                                    **jumping**
from one foot to the other, leaping or jeté;
from one foot to the same, hopping or temps levé;
from one foot to two and two to one, assemblé and sissonne;
from both to both, sauté;
all manner of variety and combination.

Jumping is three-parted
take off, flight, landing.
You can pay attention to each part.
      In the opening of Kylian's **Sinfonietta**
      flight is the supreme emphasis.
      Landings that roll, landings that slide
      are what Vandekeybus chooses for **La Mentira.**

Try jumps from less usual situations.
Jump from kneeling, jump onto your hands,
bump along on your seat.
Elevate, fly, prance, hop.
Just leave the ground and return
your way.

Turning this way and that                                                      **turning**
en dedans and en dehors,
turn this far only or on and on and on.
Turn away and turn to face.
Pirouette on one foot, rotate on two,
spin round on your seat, slew round on your knees,
just move around your own body's axis.
Virtuosic spins are a favoured choice in the ballet repertoire
sometimes for sheer bravura.
      Not so for Ulysses Dove
      who makes them his trade mark
      in **Dancing on the Front Porch of Heaven.**

Losing and re-gaining equilibrium.                                    **over-balancing,**
Feel the lability as you lose the vertical line.                        **re-balancing**
Feel the balance point as one move over-balances into another
not out of control entirely
but with enough loss to feel the danger.
Feel the momentum and the flow.

Then feel the groundedness of re-balancing,
re-finding the vertical.

**holding still**

Holding still is more than stopping.
It is continuing the state just arrived at
whatever that may be
with whatever quality
with whatever intention.
An isolation will be framed by a body holding still.

**mixtures and phrases**

Try mixing these actions :
    transfering as you turn
    over-balancing into a travel
    turning in the flight
    off-balance jumping
    holding still half way through a transfer of weight.

Try a phrase of
transfer, turn, jump, jump, travel, hold still, over-balance,
transfer while turning.
Find a second version of it
and a third.
Start it once from kneeling
once from one foot
once from sitting on a chair.

**actions for part of the body as well as the whole body**

Here are some actions commonly used.
There are only certain things the body can do -
bend, stretch, twist and tilt.
    Bending, (flexing, contracting, crouching, shortening) -
    just in your hand it makes a fist.
    Extending (straightening, stretching, expanding) -
    try it in the leg.
    Twisting (spiralling, turning in, turning out, rotating in and
    around the spine).
    Tilting (leaning, moving a limb from one joint) -
    tilt your head, move your arm in one piece.
Two more actions are commonly used by the limbs
in which bending or extending with twisting and tilting combine.
No simple terms exist for them except:
    gathering (curving gesture inward),
    scattering (curving gesture outward).

Try all these actions as a dancer.
Recognise the action content.
It will help you articulate,
give you an action intention.

Then find the motivation in the body.
Where does the bend start ?
Is it a curl in from an extremity
or a contraction from the centre ?
Where does the twist begin ?
Into what bit of you does it continue ?
And so forth.

Try them out as a choreographer.
Give yourself a row of actions,
a string of them
like beads.
Work to find the transitions from one to the next.
Work to cut out redundant moves.
Make several versions of the same row
to make material A B C.
Structure them, intermix them, counterpoint them.

Use them
to vary a vocabulary that you customarily use.
Take folk dance, street dance, clubbing,
and make it your own
as Balanchine did with ballet,
by changing its action content
radically or through small artculations.
Try over-balancing the vocabulary
as Tharp has.

**reading**

**Ann Hutchinson Guest**

Your Move, A New Approach to the Study of Movement and Dance (1983)

Since actions are what notators write this book written by a leading Labanotator discusses them in some detail. Her particular perspective takes actions apart and discusses how they might be explored.

**Valerie Preston-Dunlop**

Dance Words (Part Three: Movement) (1995)

The point of view of several artists and writers on the action part of dance is collected here.

**Merce Cunningham with Jacqueline Leschaeve**

The Dancer and the Dance (1985)

While this book covers many aspects of Cunningham's working process some time is given to his direct use of actions in his movement material, in such works as **Torse.**

# eukinetics : the study of the dynamic qualities of rhythm
## what are rhythm and dynamics made of in dance movement ?

Rhythm and dynamics
are words for aspects of movement that are difficult to discuss,
for they are felt experiences not thought ideas
and thence incompatible with words.

Because daily class is organised in counts                    **rhythm**
it is easy for dancers to believe
that rhythm means counts.
Counts are only a way of dealing objectively with time
in such a way that people can keep together,
dancer with dancer,
dancer with musician.

Metric rhythms, three-four, two-four, eights, fives
are ways of organising time and dynamics
into countable and writeable units.
Within the framework of counted time
there are movement rhythms and dynamic qualities.

Movement rhythm can be metricized.
By itself it is something else
not remotely connected to metre.
Movement rhythm arises from our experience as sentient
kinetic beings.
We have regular rhythms in our bodies
through the heart beat, through breathing, through walking,
all three open to disruption.
We have irregular rhythms in our bodies
through the tasks that we undertake,

through the expressive gestures we make to each other,
through the rhythms of speech and emotion.

Change creates rhythm.
Put any two things beside each other and
the potential for rhythm is present.
Connect any two movements
and a rhythmic form commences,
a time rhythm, a weight rhythm, a flow rhythm
or a space rhythm.

**time**

Pace... how fast the movement is, as a whole,
moderato, vivace, slow.
Duration... how long it takes,
long, short, five seconds,
how long each part feels - brief or drawn out.
Speed... how fast each move is - quick, slow,
how fast each movement feels - speedy or leisurely.
Acceleration / deceleration... the changing speed
within a movement,  within a phrase,
hurrying up, slowing down.
The feel of speeding it up suddenly,
the feel of slowing it down, sustaining it longer.

Take any movement material you know
and work with its timing
as mentioned.
Its innate time life will emerge,
or you could imbue it with an entirely new life time.
You could work with the timing of the phrase as a whole
and of the time changes within a move.

**weight and energy**

Accenting...
by giving weight to a moment in a movement -
by using gravity,
by raising the energy level against gravity,
by strengthening the movement,
by lightening a moment.
You can accent through force, through delicacy,
through weightiness, through size.

Time / Weight possibilities
are the core ingredients of movement rhythm.
How these ingredients are put together and phrased,
how the resulting movements merge or are separated,
requires flow.

**flow**

Flow ... free flow and bound flow.
Continuous flow allows one move to follow another without a break.

Its dynamic content is smoothed over.
Its rhythmic excitement is muted.
Free flow is more than continuity.
It is overflowing.
It could lose control.
Interrupted flow keeps stopping the movement's energy.
Binding the flow of energy, withholding it, may upset rhythm.
It is careful.
It can over-control.
It can destroy the flow,
but it can colour the rhythm, articulate it, briefly.

Impulsive flow accents the start of the movement
which flows on into the next.
Impactive flow accents the end of the movement,
the arrival point.
You can break the flow impactively
or bounce out from it freely.
Swinging flow may be pendular
using the momentum of weight,
or deliberately accented in the middle of the movement
to move it on with swing.

The dynamic range                                                **range**
that a choreographer requires from the dancers
marks his work.
An ff for Mozart and ff for Stravinsky
are at two different places on the sonorous continuum of
soft to loud.
Dynamic extremes required by Forsythe in **Love Songs**
would be fffff for Siobhan Davies in **White Man Sleeps**
where fluidity is often combined with a subtle range of
dynamic change.

It takes a while for young dancers
to allow themselves
to reach the extremes of strength, of slow motion,
of sudden accent.........
They think they have reached it when there is a long way to go.
The barrier may not be kinetic or technical
but sheer inexperience
for extremes require a high level of personal commitment,
even abandonment,
and that is sometimes scary.

You could use these eukinetic elements                  **using dynamics**
to become dextrous in dynamics and rhythm.                  **and rhythm**
Start with a phrase of actions,
explore its timings - sense them.

Add weight and energy - sense them.
Alter the flow - sense it.
Go for some extremes in the range.

In the end you have to stop thinking
and allow the rhythmic life of your movement to emerge.
Then you will find what Laban called effort rhythm.

Mastery of these things
does not happen over night.
As Graham said,
"It takes.......................................................time".
The possibilities are infinite,
irrreducible to words.
The challenge for the dancer
is to find the expressiveness
inherent in whatever rhythm and dynamic range is on offer.

**reading**

### Laban, Rudolf
Mastery of Movement 3rd Ed. (1971)

Laban's fundamental analysis of movement rhythm under his term "effort
rhythm" is the most comrehensive approach to date towards understanding
rhythm as a felt experience and a mode of human expression.

### Valerie Preston-Dunlop
Dance Words (Chapter : Dynamics and Timing of Movement) (1995)

The collection of statements by dance artists, writers and teachers, gives an
overview in some detail of the breadth of approaches to rhythm, dynamics,
timing and phrasing, as practiced in the dance profession.

# breath, organic and arbitrary rhythms
why do choreographers chose certain
kinds of rhythmic organisation
for their work ?

Inhale and exhale.
Feel the rise and fall of breath.
Feel the length of a breath.
Feel the suspension at the peak of the inhale.
Feel the release as the breath flows out,
the push as the last breath is forced out
and inhale again
in a continuous cycle.

**breath rhythm**

Breath rhythm in dance material is not actual breathing, always.
It is the suspension and release or
suspension and fall or
suspension and push
reflected in the rest of the body.
Suspensions occur throughout the body, not only in the lungs.
The upper arms feel them most easily,
the thighs do as they lift,
the breast bone, the top of the head.
The fall comes through dropping the weight,
letting the centre of gravity go, as if exhaling,
flowing on into the next breath cycle.

You need to be able to find the natural breath rhythm
of dance material.
Take a phrase of actions and find its breath.
You may puff in and out to start with.
Let the breath be heard.

This is just what Brumachon does in **Naufragés.**
The desparate actions of drowning
are seen and heard
as the breath is engulfed.
No music, just gasps.

When you are dancing full out
in a performance
you have to use your actual breath to stay alive
so you reflect the breath rhythm of the material
in your whole body.

Emotions cause the regular in out
to be spasmodic.
The inhale and exhale may come in gasps.
The breath can be held.
It can be shallow and short or deep and profound.
All of them can be reflected
in the life of the breath rhythm of the dance material.
If you want to bring out the emotive quality
then organise the rhythm
through its disrupted breath content.

Some material is just not breath rhythm material.
Its rhythm is based on a different principle.
Recognise that. Do not try to give it what it does not contain.

**organic rhythm**

Organic rhythms arise
through the connection of one movement to the next,
through the natural preparation-action-recovery rhythm of
movement.
One move acts as the preparation of the next.
Its recovery becomes, in its turn, the preparation for the third,
and so on.
Try it.
Taking classical material, perhaps a pirouette is one way to try.
You prepare, turn and recover to stop,
or make the recovery into a preparation for something else.

Each movement has the potential for more than one organic
connection.
The art lies in feeling / sensing
the contents of a movement,
its plurality
and using them.

The step of a move can lead into the next move
by the law of natural compensation.
An open step could lead into a closing or a crossing move.

The right arm of the same move
could lead into something quite different.
It is a matter of choice.
Out of each move
there are usually at least three possible organic follow-ons.

It is all a matter of kinaesthetic awareness
and intention to focus
on one part of the movement or another,
and then allowing the body's natural propensity for balance
to tell you what to do and where to go next.
Once again......... "It takes
...................................................................time"
You have to learn to feel kinaesthetically.

Arbitrary rhythms                                                    **arbitrary rhythm**
first arose out of attempts to find new ways of moving
by cutting across the natural rhythms of a sentient body,
a feeling person.
Chance techniques were introduced
as a means of diverting movement to new connections
by disrupting the natural energy flow.
Away with breath and organic compensation
for they tended to produce movement that had become
predictable.

Chance durations, chance actions
danced by a chance co-ordinated body
into chance derived directions, and chance sizes, were tried.
Arbitrary rhythms emerge through this method
out of the arbitrary juxtaposition of movements.

Arbitrary rhythm is sometimes referred to as action rhythm        **action rhythm**
being the innate rhythm that must emerge
from a given set of arbitrary actions.
        Such is Cunningham's way.
        He wants no search for a natural breath rhythm,
        no added dynamic colours of energy, flow and timing,
        no organic transitions.
        He needs the dancer to give
        enough time
        enough energy
        enough flow
        to do what has to be done
        in the allotted space
        for the allotted time.

Giving life to movement with an arbitrary rhythm
is hard for some dancers.

You just have to intend to do,
not to feel, not to colour,
to sense but never to dramatise or to imagine.
The enjoyment is kinetic.

**reification and rhythm**

Reducing the dancer from a fully alive person
to a moving object
can happen.
It may occur through seeing the dancer as an instrument
rather than a fully creative collaborator.
It may occur through the choice of rhythm.

Performing arbitrary and action rhythms
does not require dancers to make use of
all of their creative faculties.
These rhythms require a specialised intention,
an attentiveness to the material
rather than an expressiveness with it.
Facial expression is muted.

Arbitrary rhythms are not natural to a breathing sentient person.
Spectators pick that up.
They may see the material as mechanical,
as object like.
They may see the muted facial expression
as expressionless.
The result is a reification of the dancer.

**reading**

**Doris Humphrey**

The Art of Making Dances  (1959)

This is the standard description of breath rhythm, introduced by Humphrey and
continued through Limòn to to-day.

**Richard Kostelanetz**

(Ed) Merce Cunningham / Dancing in Space and Time (1992)

A description of Cunningham's approach to rhythm arising from the actions to
be danced is embedded in an account of his philosophy and practice.

**Valerie Preson-Dunlop**

Dance Words (Chapter : Dynamics and Timing of Movement)
and (Section on Reification in Chapter : The Performer) (1995)

Here are statements on various approaches to rhythm and reifying the dancer by
practitioners in the dance domain.

# metric rhythm
## counting and the dancer

Metric rhythms
are those in which time is cut up into measured units.

The beat is the even repetition of the units
one two three four, or one two, or one two three
that underlie the more complex rhythmic patterns of the
melody
and the rhythmic play that is around and over the beat.
It is the beat that is counted and felt as a pulse.

Time signatures
are the statement of the number of beats grouped together :
in triple time (three four time, six eight time)
in duple time (two four and four four time)
in five four or seven four time
or any other mix of twos and threes.

Triple time, waltz time, is a swinging metre.
It encourages movement flow and momentum.
Duple time, march time, emphasizes the pulse.
It encourages a more positive, active movement rhythm.
Uneven rhythms, fives and sevens
are restless, made up of one triple and one or more duple.
You can't settle to a steady pulse or a steady swing.
You have to keep shifting between the two.

Metric rhythms play around beats and time signatures.
Music uses note values.
Dance uses music's metric terminology.
Quarter notes are the staple value,
half notes are longer, over two beats,

eighth notes are shorter, over half a beat,
sixteenth even shorter.
I learnt them as ta, ta, ta, ta
ta-aa, ta-aa,
ta te, ta te, taffa teffe, ta.

**dancing metrically**

What the dancer has to do in the first place is
to feel the pulse
and go with it,
feel the triple swing and flow with it.
Every social dancer, folk dancer, tap dancer knows how to do that.
Some  people have problems with metre.
They just do not feel the pulse naturally.
Tap dancing has proved to be a useful remedy.
Hearing yourself hit the beat tells you how you are doing.

> Jazz dance is one kind of metric dance
> where use of syncopation and fragmented body
> co-ordination combine.
> Take the dances in the musical **A Chorus Line.**

**working with
metric music**

Some ways of dealing with metric rhythm are :
synchronise with the music,
syncopate the music,
counterpoint the music.
Try mixing metres,
try different metres simultaneously, one in the music,
one in the dance.
Work the movement independently
and then discover how to tie in with the music.
In each case your movement has to pay attention to metre
and also
be based on movement rhythms.
Otherwise
the movement will be reduced to redundant
counted music visualisation.

Metric movement rhythms use exactly the same ingredients and
qualities as
breath rhythms, organic and effort rhythms
except that time has one more layer.
It is measured, quantified,
constrained by counts and beats.

There is a danger for dancers
always used to working with music,
unused to working without it.
They may rely on the musical metre,
on the energy and flow and accents of the music,

following it,
so turning themselves into dependent artists,
second order artists.
If you take the music away
they can't start.
They can't find their own energy, their own effort,
their own flow and timing.
They cannot function as first order creative artists
making their own original rhythmicised material.

If you are going to work with music
as a choreographer
spend some rehearsal time without it,
without thinking about the sound,
without counting,
allowing the movements' effort, breath,
organic rhythmic life to emerge.
Then return to the music
and partner it.
Do not depend on it.

    Michèle Anne de Mey does not depend in **Love Sonnets,**
    the video version of her **Sonata 555.**
    The piece is site dependent.
    The site is Catalonia.
    It offers her two kinds of rhythmic source
    one from engaging with the Catalan countryside,
    one from linking into the indigenous Catalan dance.
    Running, rolling, falling in the dusty clay,
    scrambling over the scree,
    gives her unmetred action rhythms
    which she balances with more metred step dancing with Scarlatti.
    Then she catches the flavour of the Flamenco dance
    with its characteristic rhythmic base.

Since Stravinsky's compositions for dance,                    **irregular rhythms**
epitomised in his **Rite of Spring**
with Nijinsky's choreography,
irregular metric music has been part of dance.
Bartok's shifting rhythms based on folk dance
are irregular.
Brief bars of twos and threes, fives, sevens,
in musical dance accompaniments
make it almost essential that dancers count.
You cannot feel so many changes with certainty.
You may have to confirm the feeling with counts.

Irregular rhythms need not be music derived.
Tap dancing, Irish step dancing, clog dancing

make their own rhythmic patterns,
arising from the feet,
both seen and heard.
Although usually metric
innovators have developed irregular audible dancing.

Composers like Messaien
who use accumulated rhythmic patterning
have inspired choreographers to use accumulation
as a compositional device -
a pattern, a pattern plus, a pattern plus plus.........

Indian and African dance rhythms,
metric and tied in with their accompanying sound,
make Western dance rhythms look tame.
The foot movements of the dancers,
the hand movements of the percussionists
mirror each other, counterpoint each other,
in intricate metres.

**reading**

**Katherine Teck**
Ear Training for the Body (1994)

Although Teck is discussing music for dances she does it from the point of view
of the dancer's experience and covers metric rhythm.

# one collection of dynamic qualities
## specific qualititative actions

What is provided here
are seven dynamic actions
to be used in variety.
Each is regarded as a dance colour.

The first colour is pulsing.                                              **pulsing**
It gives a beat and a regularity.
The pace can be your own decision.
Its small vertical quality gives it an energy.
The pulse takes place in whatever movement you chose -
pulsing walks,
pulsing twists,
pulsing jumps.

Vibration is staccato,                                                    **vibration**
usually applied in short sporadic bursts.
It is excited, small, shaking.
Most obviously it occurs in the peripheries,
but a vibratory walk,
a vibratory central shiver,
vibrating shoulders
are telling statements.

A swing usually drops and lifts.                                          **swing**
It can also swing over your head
or out in front.
You can swing down to the floor.
You can swing into a jump.
It lilts in a walk.
It gives momentum into a turn.

**sustained**

Sustained is uninterrupted continuity,
not necessarily slow but continuing at the same speed.
It makes a fine contrast to the brevity of vibration
and the regularity of pulse.

**collapse**

Falling, losing energy, giving in, collapsing.
The whole body gives in to the floor.
Or only part of the body collapses,
the body giving in but not entirely.
The heavy downward quality
gives a negativity to the movement.

**percussive**

A ballistic, thrusting quality.
It can interrupt a movement
or complete one.
Several percussive interjections can fragment a movement.
It has strength.
It can be aggresssive.

**swaying**

A slow to and fro movement quality
on the horizontal plane,
contrasting with the pulse's vertical ingredient
and the downwardness of a collapse.

**strings**

Making strings and phrases of these qualitative movements
is the next step.
What emerges is like a painting of pure colours,
this colour next to that one.
These qualities are also used
to sharpen the colour of material initiated by other means -
a narrative, an image, a response to a painting.

**transitions**

These seven dynamic qualities
are a collection chosen initially by one pioneering woman,
Margaret H'Doubler.
They constitute a personal choice, her vision.
Similarly Humphrey's vision
of sharp and smooth
constituted her dynamic basis.
Both can be expanded.

Sensing how each quality might dissolve into another,
using a full range of available actions with each quality,
using several spatial forms with each are possibilities.
What happens
if you dance them while holding on to someone else ?

**H'Doubler and Laban**

Looking at how these qualities relate
to the more fundamental dynamic elements in Laban's effort rhythm

one can see that both his and hers
(and Humphrey's, and Graham's contraction and release)
are clusters of time-weight-space-flow.

The approach of each is not the same.
Laban understood movement as colourful phrases
with a fluctuating weight rhythm, time rhythm, space rhythm,
flow rhythm.
H'Doubler describes instances of defined colour
juxtaposed with other colours
which might or might not turn into a phrase.
Laban's dynamics
arise out of the observation
of the rhythm of mundane human movement,
both functional and expresssive.
They start there and become dance, become art.
H'Doubler's are indirectly connected with the mundane.
She started with dance.
The seven qualities might refer to behaviour
but they belong in the domain of pure art.

Jiri Kylian uses instances of clear colouring in **Obscure Temptation.**
Primarily a woman's solo danced by Sabine Kupferberg,
it juxtaposes one dynamic quality with another
in one nonsequitur after another.
Vibration and sustained are the dominant colours
with impulsive motion and pulsation added.

What the temptation in this dance might be we never know.
The obscurity of it and its intensity are evident.
Kylian's colourings in this work
go against the tendency in normal behaviour
to balance one colour with another,
to fade one colour into another.
This never happens.
One colour leaps in to interrupt another.

Kylian adds further juxtapositioning
through extremes of facial expression
which emerge and disappear
during phrases of movement that are otherwise formal.

The dance confounds the rules of sane behaviour.
Such contradictions of dynamic quality and of face
are eloquent of a soul sorely tried.
The message is given to the spectators
primarily through these dynamic choices
and through an articulate performance
by Sabine Kupferberg.

# rhythm, dynamics, and meaning
are rhythm and dynamic forms in
dance just forms or do they mean
something ?

The rhythms of the human being in daily life                                        **rhythms**
are naturally harmonic,
slow with fast, stillness with activity,
up leading into down, in goes out
and so on.
We have an in-built rhythmic harmony of balancing opposites.
It acts as a code by which we recognise
sanity, health and stress in each other.

Spectators bring this code with them.
They look at dance with the code of harmonic counter-balance
as a norm,
with an eye to recognise
sanity, humanity,
distress, disharmony, inhumane behaviour.

They bring with them feelings.
They know what smooth fluidity feels like,
what jagged interruption feels like.
They recognise when humans are treated like objects
through the rhythms imposed upon them.
They see it happening to dancers
through the rhythms they use in their dance.

It is the kind of rhythm used that tells them.
Breath rhythm speaks of feelings,
edging towards emotional feeling.
Organic rhythm speaks of healthy function.
Arbitrary rhythm speaks of objects moving.

Effort rhythms speak of people intending.
Metric rhythms, when they are felt, speak of the the pulse, the blood.
Metric rhythms of music, leaned on by dancers
speak of dependency.
Slow motion timing breaks with reality.
It speaks of a dream-like event.
It exposes detail disproportionately.
These meanings are on offer.
Whether they are taken in by the spectator is another matter.

**dynamic qualities**
**and psychic function**

Dynamic qualities
like colours
are not meaningless but meaningful.
The motion factors themselves represent or illustrate
the functioning of the psyche
because when we behave
our bodies reflect activity in our psyche.
They are the embodiment of the psyche.

This is one way in which we read other people's behaviour.
It is one way in which we may read meaning in dances.

The psyche, says Jung,
has four functions
with which we interact with people and the world around -
physical, mental, emotional, intuitive functions.
Behaviour is seen through four motion factors
weight, space, flow and time.
They correspond, says Laban.

It is difficult to understand this correlation through words,
much easier by experiencing it and seeing it.
But I have to try.

Take the flow - emotional correspondence…
Broadly put
freely flowing movement and bound movement
reflect the basic emotional poles of loving and hating.
The feelings of lovingness suffuse the body and flow out of it.
The feelings of hate make you tight and knotted.
Emotional feelings
are not reflected in the continuity aspect of flow
but in the inner attitude of fluidity and freedom
that the dancer gives to the material.
Hating is not reflected by the stopping aspect of the material
but by the bound inner attitude of the dancer.

This correlation needs to be more lengthily verbalised
to be anything other than a glimpse.

To start with, the words love and hate are inadequate,
for feelings merge into one another and are not separable so simply.
Neither is movement.
Nevertheless a dancer dancing fluid material
with moments of outpouring flow
will give off emotionality.
You do not have to mime emotional content.
It is given by the movement's dynamic quality.

The connection between mental clarity and spatial clarity
is easy to see.
A dance that is overtly spatially organised
gives off organisation
and that is a mental function,
thought out.

The connection between physical engagement with the world
and the weight factor in movement
is not hard to see.
The muscularity, the energy,
the will power to move with strength
is clearly more physical than mental or emotional.
Moving with lightness of touch is sentient.

The connection of time with intuition
is confusing if time is mis-thought of as counts
which are cerebral.
Timing, sudden flashes of acceleration,
playing with slowing down and speeding up,
is not rational but intuitive.
It is experienced phenomenally.

Of course these things mix.
At macro level they occur in whole sections of a dance.
At micro level they occur within one phrase
even within one movement.
The crux is that where a dancer exhibits inner attitude and intention
evidence of involvement of the human psyche is present.
Where a dancer does what has to be done, just that and no more, disengaged,
then what is given off is an unemotional, unintuitive, unmental act,
with no physicality.

This connection can work for spectators in so-called abstract dances
which appear to mean nothing
but convey something.
In narrative dances
the messages referring to events, story, characters are strong.

They may wipe out the more delicate meanings of the psyche.

Spectators may miss it all
by having their own agenda,
their own imagination.
Notwithstanding such a possibility,
the choreographer may include these things in the work.

Ulysses Dove included them in
**Dancing on the Front Porch of Heaven.**
The work is about the loss of people loved.
He is categoric :
"Dance is about form,
dance is about feeling."
Making dances is what makes him human, he said.
His psyche and his body,
his intuition, his emotion, his mental faculties all work
to create feeling and form.

The male duet "Friendship" exemplifies.
It is architectural,
weight sharing with spatial form and time changes.
No narrative unfolds.
The richness of friendship is explored
in his forms
and danced with feeling.

**reading**

**Rudolf Laban**

Mastery of Movement 3rd Ed. (1971)

Laban does not mention directly his indebtedness to Jung's work on the psyche.
Without using Jung's term 'the psychic functions' he correlates the motion
factors with the way the psyche functions in the world. They are the evidence of
that functioning.

**Jung, Carl G.**

(ed) Man and His Symbols (1964)

In this book the four psychic functions are just one of Jung's research outcomes
amongst a much wider view of his psychological studies.

## choreutics : the study of the dancer's space

how does a dancer relate to space ?
what are space-in-the-body and the
body-in-space ?

Space is an empty, amorphous void
until given boundaries,
until objects are placed in it,
until people enter it.
Then it begins to have properties
like height and depth,
like walls and openings,
like foreground and background.

**space**

The body-in-space
is the basic sculptural element of choreography.
Bodies enter and move through, in, and with a space
turning the void into a place.

**the body-in-space**
**space-in-the-body**

For bodies to become sculptural
they have to be designed,
to take on spatial properties
like horizontal and vertical, curve and straight,
void and solid, direction and focus.
This is space-in-the-body.
These two,
the body-in-space and space-in-the-body,
constitute the subject matter of choreutics.

The space can be transformed by the way the dancers
engage with it.
The word is "engage"
for dancers do more than move in space.

**engagement**

They inhabit space.
It becomes a place.
They relate to it and enliven it, bring it to life.
They command it.
It happens or it doesn't through the dancers' presence,
their sense of self presentation.

There are dancers who move about
unaware of themselves as holding choreutic properties,
unaware of their power to command the space.
There is a difference between feeling your own dancing
and feeling yourself dancing in and with the space.
That is a difference to be discovered.

Once a dancer enters the space
it becomes an arena of tensions.
Virtual lines that seem to intersect through and around the dancers
draw the spectator's eye.

Engagement with the spatial properties
in the movement material in the dancer's body,
knowing it, feeling it, intending it,
is the dancer's choreutic responsibility.
The geometry of the forms the dancer dances,
the counterpoint with other dancers spatially,
the counterpoint with the properties of the space they are in,
the geometry of the set and of the site
is what a choreographer comprehends.

These are the potential choreutic content of the performance,
of the communication.

**reading**

**Gaston Bachelard**
The Poetics of Space (1994)

Bachelard, a phenomenologist, is concerned with the meanings inherent in particlar spaces, such as a corner or a drawer, an attic or cellar. He reminds us that as soon as space is bordered it has a poetic to be experienced and engaged with. We have to apply that to the kinesphere and a performance space.

**Valerie Preston-Dunlop**
Dance Words (Chapter : Space-in-the-body and The Dancer in Space) (1995)

Statements by dance people on this topic are presented, from critics, historians, choreographers and teachers.

# maps of the kinesphere
## an exploration of the primary highways
## and the secondary pathways
## in the kinesphere

The sphere
within reach around each dancer
and in which movement is made
is the kinesphere.

Psychologists call it the personal space,
a domain belonging to the individual
as personal to him as his body.

Sociologists call it a territory
to be defended from invasion
or shared by invitation.

Each kinesphere is set apart from the general space
in which everyone else is situated.
Each dancer's kinesphere stays with her,
travelling with her wherever she goes.
Each kinesphere has a centre,
each dancer has a centre.
Directional energies stream out from that centre
through motion, through focus.

Energy can go anywhere
but
it prioritizes certain directions.
Vertical is primary.
Sensing the line through the spine
upwards to infinity, downwards to the floor, grounded,
is primary.
Equilibrium depends on a sense of the prime directions.

**kinesphere**

**dimensional directions**

The body's three dimensional compass
radiates out to right and left
to forward and backward,
intersecting with the vertical.

Sensing the primary directions as placement is important -
lateral sensing,
awareness of flank and ears as directionally sideways,
of shoulder line and lateral body symmetry,
of out-turned knees in second position.
Breadth is what it is.
Broad is what it feels.

Try sagittal sensing of forward and backward,
of advancing,
of chest, face, nose as forward directional forces.
Try retreating,
sensing the back, the nape of the neck, the shoulder blades,
as backward directional forces.

The primary highways are
up and down, right and left, forward and backward
as we all know.
Because the body is symmetric
right and left become open and across,
the arm reaching across the chest,
the leg stepping across the other leg
into the crossed over half of the kinesphere,
the half often ignored in some dance styles.

**three planes**

Joining up the six dimensional compass points
like three circular horizons
gives us the three primary planes -
the door plane (lateral plane)
the wheel plane (sagittal plane)
the table plane (horizontal plane).

**diametral directions**

The in-between locations on each plane,
those in-between the prime directions,
join together in intersecting crosses, one to each plane.
They give twelve vectors ending in twelve locations -
the diametrals.
They form a second map of the kinesphere.

**map choices**

Danse d'école
selects certain primary directions,
gives names to positions in them,
first position, second position, fifth, fourth,
and eschews the rest of space.

Early modern dance pioneers -
Graham, Humphrey, Laban, Wigman,
favoured the obliques
and the directions only reachable
by spiralling, leaning and falling
to complement the stable directions of ballet.

Because of daily class                                          **spatial imagination**
and the primary compass directions used there,
dancers can get indoctrinated
into using only those,
forgetting, or unaware of, the wealth of obliques, diagonals
and even space itself.

Spatial imagination is difficult for some people.
It can be a blind spot.
It is also a matter of seeing not only an arm moving
but the line in space that the arm leaves behind,
its itinerary.
It is a matter of being able to envisage an itinerary,
before it actually happens,
and create with that vision.
That is spatial imagination.

We need to see the patterns we make as we move
(which disappear as soon as we have made them)
but remain as a memory trace.
We need to see the design of the arrival positions,
those momentarily held places
much easier to grasp.
They impinge more strongly on the spectator's eye
than the disappearing paths.

Some dance training emphasises positions.
You move from one known position to another.
Naming the positions rather than the moves between them
underlines positional thinking.
But dancing is moving.
It is how you get from here to there,
how you phrase it, rhythmicise it.
This is what makes designs in time and designs in the body.

The primary directions,
the dimensions and the diametrals,
are  a starting scaffold
around which the dance architecture is built.
They make a kinesphere grid,
a map to be used.

**diagonal directions**

There are tertiary directions,
the diagonals
(called double diagonals in geometry)
whose poles may be seen as the eight corners of a room,
the eight corners of each kinesphere.
Diagonals take you off-balance, spiral you, lean you diagonally
even more than the diametrals.

**choreutics**
**in choreography**

Three choreographers
show how differently choreutic content and kineshere maps
can be used.
    Trisha Brown, in **MO** (1995)
    overtly states the geometry she is using
    emphasising arrival places in diametrals and diagonals
    as well as designing pathways between the planes.
    It is a spatial work, clearly designed,
    with sections constructed of spatial counterpoint,
    as she herself says.

    Not so William Forsythe for his dancers.
    He values itineraries and  fleeting positions.
    He prefers tertiary directions to primary ones.
    He says that he visualises curves and lines
    and turns them into body motion.
    He almost hides them,
    combining them with all sorts of other material,
    movement mechanics, embodied images.
    Then he counterpoints the lot.

    Characterisation through spatial form
    was shown by Martha Graham in her classic work
    **Diversion of Angels.**
    Her three women soloists,
    each one an aspect of womanhood,
    each one experiencing love,
    are given leitmotif spatial material.
    The White Girl uses verticals and horizontals.
    The Red Girl is oblique in near off-balances.
    The Yellow Girl uses diagonal directions, fleetingly.
    Their choreutic forms speak of their personalities -
    the White Girl calm, upright, an icon,
    the Red Girl fiery, dynamic and passionate,
    the Yellow Girl playful and flirtatious.

Direction is formal
but it has strong references too
as Graham's use of it reminds us.

Choreutics training
offers you the mastery over space
and curiosity about it,
for you to use how you will,
creatively.

As a dancer
choreutic knowledge should give you the opportunity
to intend, spatially,
to complement intentions that are
rhythmical, dynamic and dramatic.

 **reading**

**Lincoln Kirstein and Muriel Stuart**

The Classic Ballet / Basic Technique and Terminology (1977)

Ballet's geometry is described and illustrated.

**Rudolf Laban**

Choreutics (1966)

This comprehensive book on choreutics by the pioneer of choreutic concepts
shows various maps of space. These fundamental ones are elaborated beyond
what is included in this chapter.

**Vera Maletic**

Body-Space-Expression (1987)

Maletic, a Laban scholar, describes and illustrates the essential maps.

**Valerie Preston-Dunlop**

Point of Departure : The Dancer's Space (1984)

The maps, as grids, are described and illustrated as an introduction to how
spatial scales, rings and strings might be danced. This is a technical book.

# designing movement
## is design purely formal
## or does it symbolise ?

The basic elements out of which movement design is made are
the curved and the straight line.

**design elements**

The elements occur overtly and geometrically
in the movement material of abstract spatial dances
as the content of the work.
They are used on individual bodies,
in group designs,
in counterpointed and random ensemble work.
They occur in gestures, in postures,
in motion and positions and floor patterns.

To communicate,
an abstract spatial work eschews the referential function.
It relies on the aesthetic
and the performative
to reach the audience.
How the choreutic content is structured,
how it is intended and performed
is utterly crucial.

The basic unit of design
is the spatial cluster of curves and straights,
constructed in a style unique to each choreographer.
Each makes a choice
as to how to cluster the elements together
according to an artistic vision,
according to a crafting preference.
There is no one way.

**design clusters**

These things are found in master works.
Lines also occur in movement material
that support content of a narrative sort.

    A classic example is
Humphrey's **Day on Earth** (1947).
The image of ploughing by the farmer
is embodied in gestures taken from the curve of the
plough-share
and the long straight line of the furrow.
The image of motherhood
is embodied in the curve of cradling
into the volume of tenderness.
The image of emotional tension
is expressed through broken lines and angular forms.

    An earlier classic example is
Nijinska's **Les Noces** (1923).
The crowns of the bridal pair in Russian Orthodox weddings
are embodied in the close, curved group forms
surrounding the bride
and the bridegroom.
The plaited hair, symbol of virginity in marriage,
is embodied in twisting step patterns on a straight line
and a plaiting group form made by the Bride's supportive friends.

Neither of these works is recent.
They are architectural choreography,
inspired and solid as a rock.
They both remain in the repertory to-day.

    For recent work Forsythe stands out
as a user of the curve and the straight.
He joins curve after curve
made by different body parts
in what may seem like incredible geometric contortions,
knotting and unknotting.
He launches off a temporary curved arrival place
allowing it to lead him anywhere.
There, he perceives afresh another launch into space
by another part of himself.

    An admirer of Laban's choreutic concepts
Forsythe comes up with his own use of them
designing continuous, decentralised clusters
interspersed with moves derived from personal images.

**design as metaphor**

Spatial design communicates.
Opposing one line with another in right angled tension
says something other than curves

which succeed one another in uninterrupted flow.
Symmetric and asymmetric design clusters
carry their own potential for meaning.
Stable grounded designs contrast with
labile off-balance designs.
Simple whole body designs in unified statements
speak with a different voice
than complex fragmented organisation.

The designs of material are metaphors.
They stand for whatever the choreographer's imagination suggests
through the relevance of the choices made
in the creation of the material.
If the designed bodies and the imagination are mismatched
the metaphor never materialises
or says something else.

Each part of the dancer's body can be designed.
The line of feet, the alignment of torso,
the tilt of head, the curve of hand,
are potential statements.
Developing an eye for design
entails looking beyond the foot, the face, the chest
to the line of the foot, the line of the face, the line of the chest
and the interaction of those lines.
How they work together is the artistry.

**reading**

**Doris Humphrey**

The Art of Making Dances (Chapter on Design) (1959)

This early book discusses and illustrates Humphrey's vision of meaningful designed bodies in choreographed works.

**Valerie Preston-Dunlop**

Dance Words (Section : Designed Movement in Chapter 9) (1995)

Statements collected in the studio and from writings are collated to explore the topic.

Since William Forsythe uses and expands Laban's choreutic ideas for his movement design any of the articles in journals on his work might give the reader some clue as to his method but it is virtually impossible to put such four dimensional complexity on paper. An attempt has been made by Frankfurt Ballett to make a CDRom on his method. If you have access to a sufficiently powerful computer system this CDRom is recommended viewing.

# ChU / Mm
(choreutic unit and manner
of materialisation)
what are actual and virtual
spatial forms in dance and how do
we dance them ?

The Choreutic Unit (ChU) is a particular curve or line,    **spatial progression**
one that is placed in space and has a size.
How the line is made plain to the spectator,
how it is danced by the dancer,
how it is made to materialise
is the Manner of Materialisation (Mm).

There are four kinds of Mm.
To understand them you have to do them
not just read about them.
Performing is the only way to make the words meaningful.

We can all trace a line in space
with an arm,
with a leg,
by a floor pattern.
The line or the curve
is never there at any one moment.
It is always en route,
being realised over time.
When the move is finished the trace has disappeared.
Yet we appreciate its existence.

It is not an actual form but
a virtual form.
We feel we have made a circle
and the spectator believes us.
It is the dancer's intention that makes the form appear
rather than making a movement happen.

Lines and curves made to appear over time in this way are
Spatial Progressions.

**body design**

Trace a curve with your arm
ending with the arm itself curved.
That is a spatial progession becoming a curved Body Design.
Trace a curve and end with the arm itself straight.
That is a spatial progression becoming a straight Body Design.
The arm will look like an arm or look like a curve (or straight)
according to the dynamic with which the intention is performed.
Mms are never automatic.
They are created by the dancer.

Trace a large curve with the arm
ending with a curved body design made by the whole body
from finger tips through arm, shoulder, torso, leg to toes.
Body Designs appear when the shape is in the flesh and bone
of the body.
It is almost actual.
It is as actual as unstraight, uncurved bones can be
for they are anatomically not geometric.
They are made to appear to be curved by the dancer.

**spatial projection**

Trace a straight line with your arm
from the body centre out into space.
Don't stop the energy at the finger tips.
Send energy out in a line beyond them.
Enliven the space beyond the fingers.
Project the energy into space.

The projection is not actual.
Nothing is there.
Yet the spectator can follow the energy line
beyond the body.
It is a virtual line
made to appear through the performance of the dancer.

Some body parts project easily -
finger tips, palms, the face, the chest,
bent elbows and knees, sole of the foot, toes.
Try projecting from the palms, upwards or forwards,
while holding your arms out sideways.
If you focus forwards down,
energy will be directed into the space from your eyes and your face.
The spectator will tune into the projection.

A body design may project or not
according to the energy with which it is made.
A spatial progression may project beyond its finishing place or not.

Curved spatial progressions project in two ways.
The first is by extending the end of the curve traced,
giving the impression it continues on its journey.
The second way is
by projecting across the line of the traced curve,
setting up an impression of occupying more space than it
actually does.
The only way is to try it.

No Mm is by any means automatic.
It is created by the dancer.
An arm swing is an arm swing
or
it is made to produce a curve.
The dancer dictates what can be seen
by the choice of manner of materialising the content.

Spatial tension is an imagined line                                    **spatial tension**
between two parts of the body
or two dancers
or between the floor and a part.
It can arise through a counter-tensioned movement.
It can arise by how two limbs are placed to relate
at the end of their concurrent movements.
A tilted or horizontal or vertical line appears,
virtually,
between the two parties.

Put your palm a bit of a distance in front of your chest.
A virtual relationship arises between the two as a spatial tension
with a directional value, maybe horizontal,
depending on where your torso is.

Clusters are groups of choreutic units                              **dancing Mm clusters**
occurring simultaneously or consecutively,
made evident
through mixes of any of the four materialisations -
spatial progression, body design,
spatial projection, spatial tension.
Discerning the Mm clusters of the material you have to dance
is extremely helpful to the performer.
It brings out the subtlety of the material.

You have to spend moving time on this material
with concentration on the forms being made,
consciously allowing projections to arise,
spatial tensions to form,
consciously articulating a body design after a progression.
That is the way to develop a choreutic facility.

Reading about it is only a partial answer.

Mms are valuable to dancers.
Being able to choose how to dance given material
by playing with the Mm content
is an artistic skill worth acquiring.
Mms are valuable to choreographers,
building up design consciousness
of both actual and virtual spatial content in dance material.
The virtual sort are often ignored or forgotten
but they make powerful material.
They feel like nuances
but in truth
they underline the pith of the choreography.

> In **In the Studio (Shapes)**
> Ton Simons uses body designs, spatial progressions
> and projections
> with infinite skill
> in all manner of clusters.
> Just that.
> No drama, no climaxes.
> Just formal material for two people
> in choreutic counterpoint.

**illusion**

If you are not into virtual elements,
if you are not into creating illusions,
if you are not into seeing the body as spatial form
then ChU/Mm may not be for you.
Let the swing be a swing.
Let the pathway be about getting somewhere.
Both are valuable ways.

If you shift from the mundane to the dream
from the real to the illusion of reality,
from bodies to abstract forms,
then as you shift
ChU/Mm is a spatial tool.

> Gillian Lynne's work **A Simple Man** about the painter Lowry
> shifts in this way.
> From an apparently haphazard crowd of people (mundane)
> organised space, time and rhythm emerge (the illusion).
> The dancers' paths,
> their spatial relationships to each other,
> the way their designed bodies interface geometrically
> makes the transition from actual to virtual.

**Valerie Preston-Dunlop**

"Choreutic Concepts and Practice"

in ~ Dance Research Vol 1 No 1 (1983)

The ChU / Mm ideas are introduced and illustrated

 **reading**

# working together
what are the kinetic tools for exploring
duo and ensemble material ?

Doing the same thing,
dancing the same material
in unison
is an elementary means of getting two or more people
to share the same space and the same time.

When one person dances alone
a spectator tends to see the person in a space
more than the movement being danced.
When two people dance the same material
the tendency is to see the material, then the differences in the people.
It is all a matter of choosing what suits the theme.

As soon as the choreographer starts to manipulate the two dancers
by changing the facing of each,
by playing with the timing of each,
then a relationship emerges and the movement recedes.
When two human beings occupy the same space
anyone watching will anticipate that they have,
or will have,
some form of relatededness.

Forms, patterns, phrases will arise by avoiding each other,          **almost touching**
sliding by,
surrounding closely,
by moving over, under, around and through another dancer's space
with all manner of actions.
The emergent relatedness through the proximity of two bodies
is dependent upon the dancers' articulation.
Will they touch or won't they ?

Body surfaces carry potential for meaning.
They are each expressive in their own way.
Almost touching can carry erotic overtones.
It can suggest claustrophobic spaces.
It can speak of secret journeys.
It can be simply itself, its articulate self.

**touching**

All manner of touching
creates strong duo and ensemble material -
touching lightly, caressing, pressing
brushing over,
moving while keeping touch.
What will be made available to the spectator
is purely formal or potentially narrative,
depending on performance.
Touching is a powerful indicator
of connectedness.

Supporting the connection
through posture and through focus,
framing it by the rest of the body,
strengthens the message.
Confounding the straightforward statement of touch
by witholding the posture,
by contrasting the direction of focus,
creates tension.
It sets up a question.

**sharing weight**

Leaning on to other people,
pulling away from them,
balancing against them,
all manner of clambering, lifting, dragging,
give off signs of physicality, of corporeal involvement,
an intimacy of some sort.
In contact improvisation
democratic duet forms emerge
with mutuality and concern for each other
as equal beings.
The dramatic content of the material is neutral.
Audiences may find them less interesting
than they are to the movers.

Uneven support
in pulling over, pushing off,
in being weighty on another person
or coping with your own kilograms,
letting go, losing equilibrium, lifting someone off their feet,
hazardous balances,
all give off power play.

Phrases using near to, weight sharing and distancing
can bring out statements of sheer beauty,
statements referring to human feeling.
Going beyond the cultural taboos of touching in dance
might give rise to a shocked response
or an amused one.
Dancers need time to resolve technical problems
inherent in partner and ensemble work,
especially with a weight content.

Creating designs together                                    **spatial relatedness**
gives off a sense of organisation,
of pre-planning.
They carry a thoughtful awareness of other people.

Reiterating another dancer's line,
confirming it, elongating it, reflecting it, continuing it
in some fashion
is a way of stating togetherness and accord.
Creating forms with contrasting spatial content -
a straight against a curve,
a stable vertical across a labile oblique,
something tight contrasted with a generous use of space
are ways of getting at involvement that has some tension.
Creating forms which complement each other
in interweaving counterpoint
gives a sense of an involvement of some complexity.

Using tasks that combine weight sharing with design making
may sharpen a choreographer's eye,
may sharpen the dancers articulation of the form of a lift,
or the design of a drag.
Performers cannot see the designs they create together,
they need an outside eye to check it out.

Structuring or improvising with time relatedness            **time relationships**
is more than playing with the timing dynamic
of each person's material.
Alternation, question and answer phrasing give off a time relatedness.
So do moments of synchrony,
so do unpredictable syncopating of each others moves.
So do metric counterpoint and counterpoint in breath rhythm.
So can a sharp sense of duration and pace of one phrase
against another.
All are possible.

Passing energy from one dancer to another                    **flow relatedness**
across the space, near by or touching,
gives off a feeling involvement with the other person.

It is different from the organised involvement of spatial designs,
different from the physicalilty of touch and weight sharing,
different from the intricacy of a time relationship.
Stopping the flow of another,
getting in the way, interrupting, disrupting a phrase
is a strong anti-social indicator.

**mixtures**

Each mode of connection
offers a starting point for creating phrases.
Layering of different modes of connection
offer a means of thickening the idea.

Most duos,
most ensembles
contain a mixture of ways of connecting.
  Hans van Manen focuses on supports in **Two.**
  His inventiveness and variety for Brigitte Martin and Johan Inger,
  within the limits he sets himself,
  hold the attention.........
  designed supports, fluid supports,
  technically demanding supports,
  supports in motion and stillness,
  unusual holds.
  His invention is tempered by well tried structuring.
  We can see repetition.
  We can recognise reiteration.
  Their performance is workman-like.
  No emotion, just articulate motion.

If only one kind of connectedness is present, only spatial perhaps,
the material would have to be exceptionally original
or exquisitely performed to hold an audience.
  Ton Simon's **In The Studio (Shapes)** is just that.
  This series of duo studies on spatial forms
  presents choreutic counterpoint with unswerving clarity.
It is performed with commitment and inner concentration.
Both the aesthetic pleasure in the forms
and the belief in the dancers' statements of them
carry the spectator along.

For dancers it is helpful
if they are given access to the choreographer's intent
in terms of the kind of connection wanted.
Then they can articulate.
Then the content can be given a sharp form.

**co-existence
and chance methods**

What is described here
is types of relatedness.
How they are structured together,

how they arise in the first place,
is another matter.
Some choreographers like to plan their ensembles in detail.
Others like to use chance.
Others like to give dancers individual material
give them a space and duration to co-exist in
and watch for the result.
It is a matter of choice.

Many a choreographer will start from dramatic fantasy
or imagination
and allow the material to emerge.
Ultimately fantasy has to be given form
spatial form, time form, weight form, flow form.

**Valerie Preston-Dunlop**

reading

Dance Words (Chapter : Some Ensemble, Group, Duo and Solo Dance
Concerns) (1995)

All manner of dance ideas on working together are compiled from the practice
and writings of professionals in the field.

Almost any book describing a choreographer's working method for ensemble
and corps pieces will give examples of their choices in principle. Many books
do not go into the detail discussed here.

# structuring movement material
are there traditional and current ways
of structuring dances ?
Does structure carry meaning ?

Dances are formed.                                                                                           **form**
Form is a technical term.
It can be mistaken as synonymous with the spatial form
but the word "form", by itself,
refers to the recognisable spatial-rhythmic-bodily units of a dance
passed on by tradition
or newly created.

Form can be looked at as hierarchic.                                               **hierarchic structure**
The dance event takes the top place in the hierarchy.
Each separate dance in the event takes the next layer.
Sections of the dance take the next layer.
Sub-sections take the next.
Phrases within each sub-section take the next.
Motifs within the phrases take the next.
Cells take the next
leaving elements as the lowest rank of the hierarchy.

Many dances are made with this structuring method.
    Take Nijinska's **Les Noces** as an example.
    It is usually given as part of a mixed programme of three works.
    It is divided into four named scenes.
    **The Consecration of the Bride,**
    **The Consecration of the Bridegroom,**
    **The Departure of the Bride, The Wedding Feast.**
    Each scene has recognisable changes of material
    which can be identified as sub-sections.
    The shift from ballet derived vocabulary
    to folk dance derived material
    to the ritual material of a Russian Orthodox Wedding
    becomes visible.

Each section of vocabulary is phrased
corresponding to the musical phrasing of Stravinsky's musical score.
Each phrase has movement motifs
consisting of several movements,
each a multiple of elements
which recur and can be manipulated.
Motifs contain cells -
two or three elements which always occur together.
Finally, single elements are identifiable.

Elements are the smallest particles of form -
an arm gesture, a transference of weight, a focus,
a stamp, a clap.

The same hierarchy functions in plays -
totality, acts, scenes, moments, words, gestures.

**seamless**

In current choreographic practice
each layer of this hierarchy is questioned.
Dances may not be divided into sections but continuous.
If they are in sections each may be of highly uneven length.
While subsections may be identified for rehearsal purposes
the spectator is given no recognisable clue as to the change
from one to the next.
Phrases may be of any length,
may contain any number of elements and cells
even fifty
or just one.
There may be no distinctive motifs made,
simply elements strung together.

**strings**

Elements are sometimes likened to beads
and strung together in strings
like a necklace.
They start somewhere, go on and end somewhere
or may be cyclic.
A string may be carefully fashioned
as the core material for a whole dance.
It is then subjected to all manner of formal devices
and so becomes a dance work.

**clusters**

Cells and motifs are sometimes linked as clusters.
They can be simultaneous clusters
in which several things happen at the same time
like a chord in music.
They can happen successively
where several things which belong together
follow each other
as sound elements do in a musical melody.

At one time certain criteria were regarded as essential
for a successful phrase.
It should have a climax of some sort within it -
at the beginning and ebb away from it,
in the middle and rise to and resolve from it,
at the end and build continuously towards it.
This kind of phrase
is associated with the phrasing of classical music
and the phrasing of traditional poetry
and the rhythms of speech phrasing.
It is more likely to serve
in works in which character is prioritized over abstract form
or in works that are danced with music.

**phrases**

The idea of tension and resolution is reflected in the
notion of climax.
Works with dramatic tension need climaxes
but not every work requires them.
Climax is used in phrases, in sections,
in whole works and whole evenings of works,
or not used at all.

**climax**

Sections of dances, traditionally, were distinct.
But they may grow out of each other imperceptibly
appearing seamless.
They may follow each other logically
or illogically
by juxtaposing contra-contextual material.
Episodic structuring of sections is used
in which a topic is explored not by narrative
but by presenting several perspectives of the same theme
in episodes, one after another.

**sections**

Kinds of structuring for a work may be deliberately chosen
or intuitively appear during rehearsal, unplanned.
It is important that the kind of structure decided upon
supports the idea.
Structure carries meaning.

**structure and meaning**

It carries meaning because
our body is our datum point for making sense of events.
Our body has inherent structures.
Our limbs are sectioned into upper and lower halves, plus hands
and feet.
Our pulse is a regular beat with time divided into elements.
Our breath, at rest, is a certain length.
Our day light is balanced by darkness.
Our emotions climax and resolve.
We don't walk backwards or upside down.

We don't speak in a sentence of fifty equally stressed syllables.

If you structure your work
according to the innate structures of a human being
you will enhance a theme of human experience.
If you structure your work
against the innate structures
then the form will not conjure human experience
but be form for its own sake.
And why not.

What matters fundamentally
is what is structured with what
as well as how they are structured together.
  Take Hans Tuerlings' extensive duo **A Noeud Couland !**
  He is consistently putting together
  things that don't belong together,
  nonsequiturs, juxta-positioning opposites,
  allowing things to co-exist that rarely do co-exist in reality.

  The piece is phrased in that the two dancers come together
and go apart
  in bit lengths that are recognisable
  but there is nothing regular in the phrasing -
  nothing that you could anticipate.
  Basically it is element after element in motifs that never repeat.
  Each element does not belong to its following element.
  Nevertheless each element arises from its preceding one
  not logically
  but illogically.
  The image of claws emerges from a formal turn,
  an image of work follows a fall,
  an image of aggression follows a slight hand gesture,
  a swing gives rise to a grooming gesture.

Because this inconsistency is consistent
it adds up to a metaphor of a complicated relationship.
You may see the interruptions and cut offs and unexpectedness
as refering to how our fragmented and unruly lives are.

Or you may see an unusually structured duet
athletic, virtuosic in its way,
just itself.
It is up to you.

**Peggy Van Praagh and Peter Brinson**

The Choreographic Art / An outline of its principles and craft (1963)

This early book outlines the traditional way of working in the domain of classical ballet.

**Sally Banes**

Terpsichore in Sneakers, 2nd Ed. (1980)

The experiments of the Judson Church group of dance makers show how the traditional values and hence modes of structuring were confronted and what innovative replacements were explored in an effort to find post Modern Dance forms.

**Valerie Preston-Dunlop**

Dance Words (Chapter : Choreographic Form) (1995)

Different kinds of dance works, their parts in both narrative and formal works, in traditional and contemporary ways of structuring are offered in statements from professionals in the field.

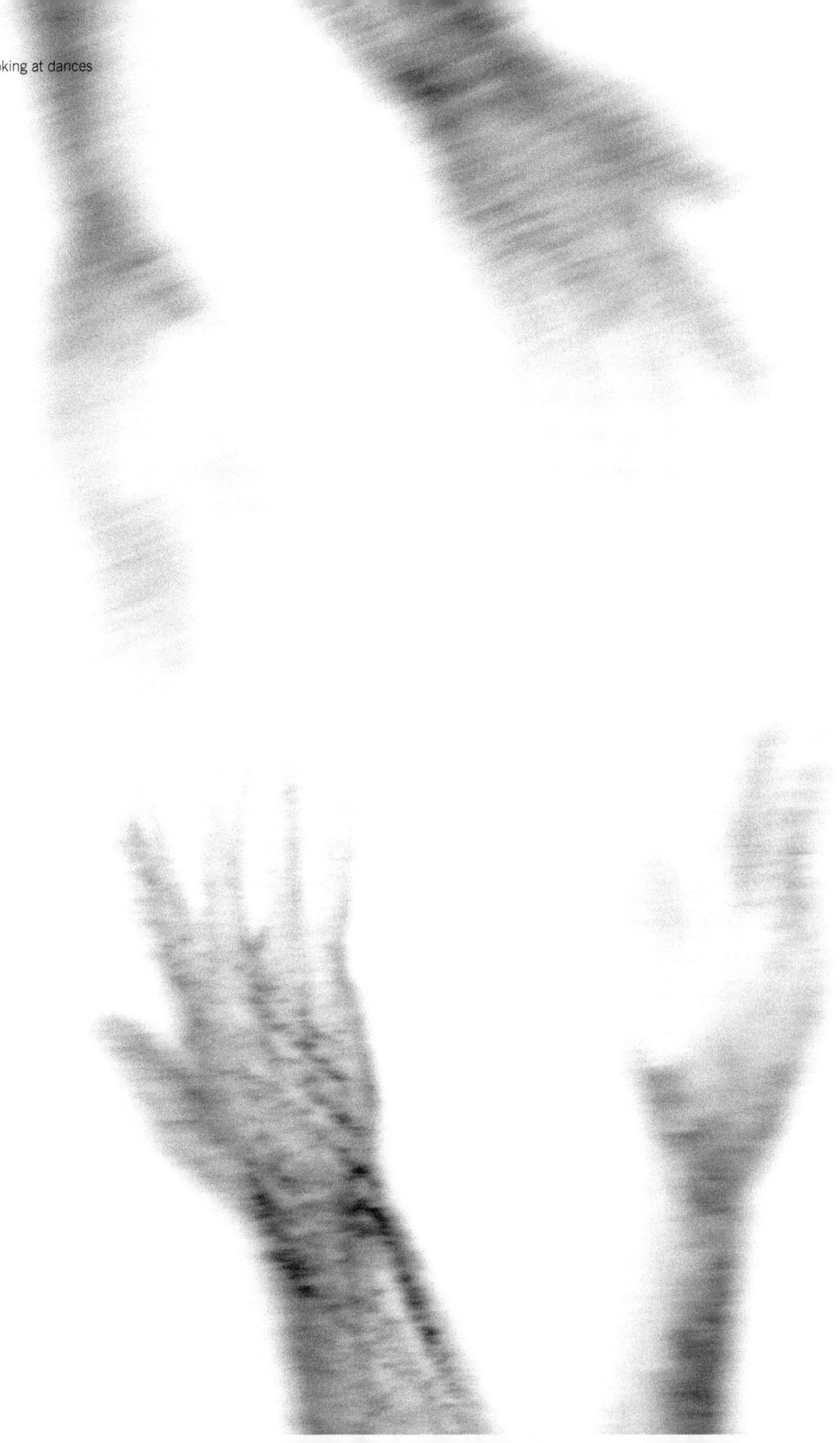

# formal devices and manipulation
what kinds of formal devices do
choreographers use ?

Once choreographers have a string of movement beads
or an extended phrase of movement cells and elements
they are in a position to manipulate them.
Manipulation has to serve a purpose.

**B material**

A second phrase may well be made
compatable with the first.
Choreographers have their own methods.
One, traditionally called ABA,
requires that the B phrase
contrasts with the A,
can be danced after the A
the subsection being completed by a return to the A material.
Rondo structuring uses B and C and possibly D material
coming back to A in between each,
ABACADA.

Theme and variation
is another traditional method
derived from the structure of classical and folk music.
Varying the thematic material
through dynamic changes, spatial changes,
number of dancers,
mood and other compositional devices
is how it is realised.
   Traditional it may be
   but it continues to be used imaginatively
   as Kristina de Chatel does in **Paletta.**
   She does it through minimalist variation techniques.

**theme and variation**

**canon**

A canon is a way of performing the string or phrase
by more than one person,
the second person starting the string
when the first person is already into it.
The entry point of each dancer is regular
in traditional methods
but need not be.
    For Dove in **Vespers**
    canon serves a clear purpose.
    Being a dance for six women
    who between them embody one woman,
    an intensely memorable woman to the choreographer,
    he needs to have a device to fragment  their unison material
    while maintaining the possibility
    to treat each dancer in turn as a soloist within an ensemble frame.

**satellites**

A second material, a satellite, can be made from the first
with the aim that the two can be danced together
to create a duo counterpoint.
The satellite material then becomes the subject of
a second satellite
and so on
until the primary phrase or string
has as many pieces of satellite material made from it
as the choreographer requires.
    This is what Trisha Brown does in **Musical Offering**
    or **MO** as she entitles it.
    She uses her eye
    and her imagination
    to structure all these strings together,
    possibly in an ensemble work,
    making use of changes of front,
    exits and entrances,
    noticing clustering and texture shifts.

**counterpoint**

The term counterpoint is used loosely or technically
to mean the layering of at least two pieces of material
so that some kind of harmonic connection between them
is formed.
Classic counterpoint is spatially derived
using some or all of the following :
    Harmonic opposite -
    movement in the opposite direction
    according to the dancer's body
    or opposite in stage direction
    so that some kind of counter-tension emerges.
    Axis and equator -
    a linear form being the axis for a curved form made around it.
    Right angled interval -

one line of energy crossing another at right angles.
Narrow interval -
two lines hitting each other or crossing each other
so that a sharp angle is made
a form sometimes full of tension requiring resolution.
Stable and labile -
the juxtaposition of balanced with off-balanced material.
Repetition and symmetric repetition.

Counterpointed structuring
can be made obvious or hidden
according to whether the choreographer wants
to facilitate the spectator's reading of the structure
or not.
If hidden, the device of displacement in time may be used.
The counterpoint material
may not occur simultaneously with its prime material
but later.
If displacement in space is used
the two counterpointing movements
are not danced in close proximity
but distanced from each other.

Counterpoint may be fragmented
like shattered glass
or light on water
in which intuition and chance play more of a part
than deliberate planning.
This is how Forsythe describes his prefered counterpointing.

Fragmentation as a structure                                    **fragmentation**
entails taking a string apart,
into single elements or motifs,
using the bits independently,
possibly reassembling them at some point
in another way or the same way.

Dancing material backward                              **retrograde and inversion**
starting at the end and proceeding to the beginning,
dancing it reversing every up to a down,
every forward to a backward
and combining these two methods
is one way of extending and developing a phrase into a section.

Starting with one piece of material                                **layering**
for the spectator to look at,
adding another, then another,
until a tapestry of material is offered
is straight forward layering.

Stuart Hopps, working in opera,
describes how he uses this method
when building up the movement material for the chorus
in massed group scenes.
Fore-grounding is a particular layering
in which certain material is prioritized for the spectator
for brief or long spans.

**sandwiching**

Sandwiching is inserting a second kind of material
into an established phrase or string.
The insertion can be of the same sort of material
or contrasted, contra-contextual,
from another kind of vocabulary.
>    Some choreographers sandwich the dancers' creative material
>    into their own string
>    which they previously fragment variously.
>    This was a prefered method by Rui Horta
>    in workshops after his success
>    at the Bagnolet Choreographic Competition.

Used with an ensemble
it is a way of combining organisation
and apparent random differences.
Elements danced by everybody at different times
are recognised and hold the group together
while the dancers own material, sandwiched,
adds individuality.

**chance methods**

Choosing material by chance methods
is a way of overcoming the limits of human imagination.
Throwing dice to choose from an index of possibilities
is the classic way.
Each user of chance methods has his own way of disrupting
the predictable.
For some choreographers, Cunningham for example,
chance takes place only in the rehearsal studio.
Its results are edited to become
determined movement material for the performance.

**indeterminacy**

When chance is used in the performance itself
the work is open to change as it proceeds.
Structures for improvisation may be put in place
while actual movements are left up to the performer.
Or - strings may be set
while exits and entrances are left up to the performer.
Or - exits and entrances may be set
but choice of which sattelite to dance is left open.
>    Rosemary Butcher found this of interest for her formal
>    ensemble pieces
>    in her seasons in London's Institute of Contemporary Art.

Choreographers using highly innovative movement
beg the question : Is This Dance ?
Spectators may be confused
because they know the rules and see that they are being
subverted.
By combining such departures
with recognisable structuring devices
the answer becomes : Yes It Is.
The structure can hold the piece together for the audience
while the choreographer plays with the codes and the icons.
Equally, innovative structuring can be used
with traditional movement material.

These apparently contradictory ways of functioning
are used highly successfully.
Bausch's Tanztheater innovations are a prime example.
The method accomodates the creative need
of the choreographer
with the reception needs of the spectator.

The essential decisions are always of the same kind -
does the choice support the central choreographic idea ?
Will it engage the spectators in the way intended ?

**contradictions**

 **reading**

**Valerie Preston-Dunlop**
Dance Words (Chapter : Section on Formal Devices) (1995)

Statements on these and further devices are given by choreographers working in
all manner of styles.

**Stephanie Jordan**
Striding Out / Aspects of Contemporary and New Dance in Britain (1992)

Amongst an all round description of her topic, Jordan uses her understanding of
the practice of choreography to outline the devices used by her selected
choreographers.

**Sally Banes**
Terpsichore in Sneakers / Post-Modern Dance (1980)

Banes gives clear description of the subversive experiments of the Judson
Church pioneers in New York in the 1960s, whose innovations have become
standard devices and are widely used to-day.

**Janet Adshead**
(ed) Choreography Principles and Practice (1987)

Papers from a conference on choreography with contributions from well known
writers on the methods of established choreographers.

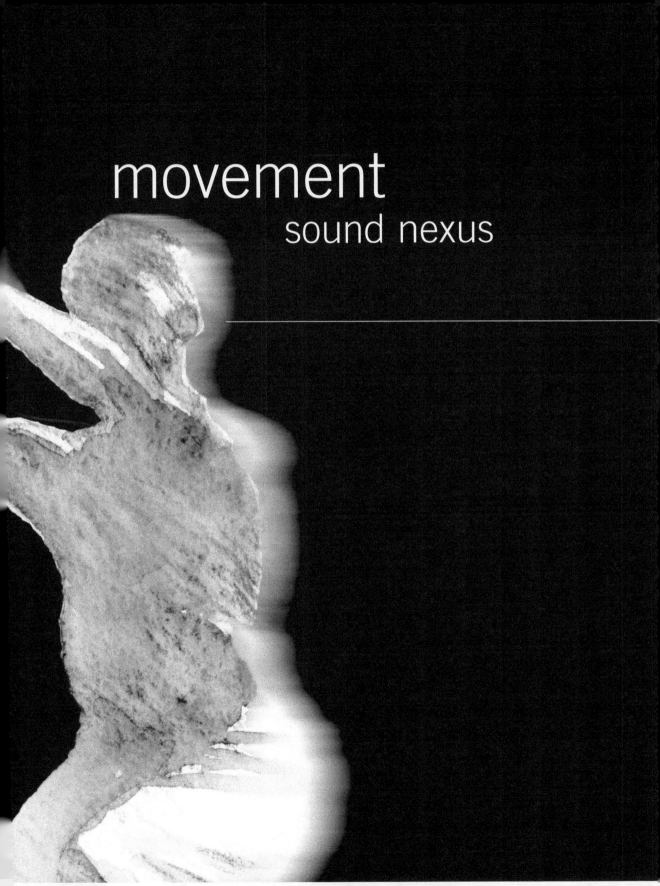

# movement
## sound nexus

# the sound of a dance
possibilities and choices in the
sound elements of a dance work

The sound of a dance is a crucial ingredient.
It carries strong messages.
It sets the mood.
It suggests a culture.
It influences the way a spectator looks at the movement.

How dance people listen to music,                    **musicians' perspective**
how musicians listen to it,
is not the same.
Performers are concerned with collaborating with it,
getting cues from it,
finding how to work with it.
The musicians' concerns are how to create it and play it,
how to hold the tempos with each performance.
The choreographer's concern is how the two interface.

Whatever the perspective,
people need to be able to handle
the technical language of their collaborating artists.
Time, pitch, timbre and amplitude
are the basic elements of contemporary sound.
Up beats, down beats, off beats, cues in the score,
musical beats and dancers' counts are not the same.
Musical phrasing and dancers' strings
may not correlate.

Music can inspire a choreographer.                    **choosing the sound**
It often does, successfully.
Music can swamp the ear of the spectator
through its decibels and its density
making a dance difficult to look at.

Music can tie you, hand and foot,
pushing you to make your dance fit its rhythms, its moods,
its lengths.

Just because you like a piece of music as music
does not mean it will suit your idea for a dance.

The sound has to be just right.
Everything,
costume, lighting, sound, venue, choreography,
must support the idea.

**pre-recorded music**

All manner of sound is heard in dance performances.
Searching for pre-recorded music
may seem the most obvious starting point.
It may prove a lengthy trawl.
It certainly has an uncertain outcome.
It is by no means the only way.

Pre-twentieth century music originally written for dance
is likely to have a definite pace,
a constraining structure,
a pervasive rhythmic base,
changes of mood
that may not coincide with
changes in a contemporary theme for a dance.
A clear strategy
on how to work with, rather than work under the sound
would be essential.
Without it the choreographer may become a second degree artist
simply interpreting someone else's originality,
rather than a primary one who creates an original statement.

**jazz and pop**

Jazz gives an energy base
but it also suggests a style.
So, too, does pop music.
However tempting it may be to use the popular sound of the day
to do so may diminish the dance
to a secondary place.
The choreographer's individuality could be reduced
to yet another popular movement arranger.
If the dance idea calls for it,
and comments on it,
then it may well work.

**cutting**

To cut the music or not
is a problematic question.
While the choreography may demand it
the music may make no sense without its full structure.

Musicians are affronted by cutting.
Music lovers recognise it and dislike it, heartily.

There are other ways than cutting.                                    **silence**
Fading in and out,
purposefully,
making a partner of the music,
entering and exiting it, as the dancers do,
is one possibility.
Bringing the sound forward in amplitude
then backgrounding it,
overlaying it with speech and with dancers' sound,
is another.
In any event, consult a musician.

There is no such thing as a silent dance
except on the TV with the sound turned down.
Musicless dances are made
but without music the dancers' own sound becomes obvious.
Then you see the rhythm of the movement.
The rhythm of music makes a stronger impact on the ear
than does the rhythm of the movement on the eye.

To decide to hear the dancers or not
is a question.
    If you share the sound of breath and footfall with the spectators
    the dancers will seem to them real, physical.
    Vandekeybus does in **Roseland,** in **La Mentira.**
The more you hide their natural noises
the more removed from reality dancers appear -
ethereal, dream-like, reified.

A so-called silent dance                                              **empowerment**
empowers the performers.
They are, and they appear, in control
of the flow of the event.
They give off autonomy.
If dancers are asked to stick closely to the music,
they become dependent, willy nilly.
Using the music in partnership
in dance / music counterpoint
provides a useful mix.
The spectator's ear is carried along,
given feeling through sound,
while the eye can take in the structures of the dance,
the power of the performers.

Shoe music, clapping, prop sounds                                    **sound mixes**
all emanating from the dancers

relieve the choreographer from the constraints
of music matching.
The success of dancers speaking, dancers singing
relies on their breath and ability to communicate.

Musical pitch, rhythm and texture reach the emotions.
Words do something else as well.
They reach the intellect.
A text can make you see a dance according to its verbal content.

Scott Johnson's sound for Itzik Galill does.
**When You See God Tell Him** is a duo
with all the things in it a good duo should have
without prioritizing originality of movement.
The text is short, fragmented and repeated.
The reiteration makes you listen and look again.
"So many things…
need to be said…
again and again…"
So we see many things again and again
and feel they need to be said.
"We are becoming…
one family…
enjoy the differences…"
We see differences, we sense different humanities.
We see becoming, growth.
We sense a oneness of the two individuals
on a universal not an intimate level.
The text guides our eyes.

Making your own sound track
is one solution but hazardous.
With digital recording
layers of sound can be stored and played with -
exiting and entering,
doubling, distorting, echoing,
retrograding, repeating, slowing down,
interspersed with patches of silence,
patches of song, of words,
of bird song, of children's voices, of clanking metal.

Such a score can be edited after the dance is made
so that length, loudness, appropriateness,
can be decided later in the creating process
rather than at the outset.

Popular songs lighten the atmosphere.
Folk music suggests an ethnic domain,
while some muzak is simply aural wallpaper.

Music choices go in popular waves.
Minimalist sound generated a following.
Liturgical singing could be heard regularly.
Brahms and Chopin had a predictable home.
Follow the vogue or go your own way.

Where sounds come from matters.
Possibly from a radio visible on the set
or from a loudspeaker behind the spectators
or stereo sound shifting around the space
or from a musician on stage
as well as from the orchestra pit.

**kinaesthetic gap**

Music or sound can overcome the kinaesthetic gap.
This gap is the abyss between the kinetic experience
of the performer
and the visual experience of the spectator.
Where it is important that the dancers' feeling is transmitted
then the sound might reinforce an accent,
or lighten a delicacy of movement.
The spectator is helped to feel
by hearing what he is seeing.

    Jiri Kylian is a master at overcoming the kinaesthetic gap.
    In **Sarabande** he does just that.
    The movement dynamic is underlined, sonorously.
    The sound of a footfall is enlarged and echoed.
    The sound of a dancer's voice is amplified and resonates.
    Every kinetic accent re-sounds.
    The spectator / auditor sees and hears
    what Kylian has to say.

Whatever the choice
it cannot avoid carrying meaning.

**reading**

**David Revill**
The Roaring Silence: John Cage A Life (1992)

Cage's collaborations with Cunningham are included in this biography.
They are cited here as an example of such collaborations written from the
musician's perspective .

**Valerie Preston-Dunlop**
Dance Words (Chapter : The Dance Sound) (1995)

Statements from the musicians' point of view on music and sound for dances
are compiled to give an overview of creating sound for dance.

# the movement / sound nexus
how do dance people work
with music ?

It is decades since simply making music visible
has been an acceptable way of choreographing.
Yet it is a method still to be found
in the aspiring dance maker's first attempts.
Until a dance person can rid himself of dependency on music
and learn to interface with it,
he limits his choices.
Opening his own mind, his body and his imagination by
interacting with the music's sonorities,
extends his horizons.

Countless master choreographers start with a musical work,
listen to it,
study its score until they know its construction,
feel with it,
until their vision of how to work with it gels.
Then they begin.

Countless others start independently
without the benefit, the prop, the constraint
of an existing sound.
They may intend to have a sound score, eventually,
but use their own ideas
to create the movement work,
or possibly the whole kinetic, visual, aural event.

Both ways offer opportunities.
Both ways have their hazards.

**working with a composer**

Starting with a composer
as Graham did with Horst for **Primitive Mysteries**
as Bruce did with Chambon for **Swan Song**
as Cunningham did with Cage, again and again,
allowed them to bounce off each other's imagination,
allowing both to influence the creative decisions
as the work proceeded.
The finished score
may not be heard until the final rehearsal
and that is scary
if you want to interact with it,
or just right
if you want to co-exist with it.

Those two concepts,
interaction and co-existence,
are two ways of working
which reflect an artistic point of view.

**co-existence**

Co-existence of the elements of the work,
the movement, the sound and the aural elements
occupying the same space and time,
is one particular nexus,
one web of relationships.
It was first used as a means of giving autonomy to dance,
of relieving it of its legacy of musical dependence.

Co-existence does more than that.
We function in the world
by co-existing with other elements
that have little or nothing to do with us.
A passing aeroplane, a stranger in the street,
a dog barking, water running, a computer purring,
and each one of us doing our thing, independently.
A theatre work that uses co-existence
reflects the mundane as it is
without forefronting any one bit of it,
or evaluating one perspective over another
or making an illusory world out of it.
Co-existence methods put it all there
to be attended to,
to be heard and seen.

Co-existence
allows the spectator to read into the event whatever he likes.
Imaginations can soar.
They can also stall.
The desire to see meaning is a human attitude.
We look for it in theatre.

We long to understand or to be moved.
We make connections that are not intended but allowed.

Deliberately putting two elements of a dance work together                    **contra-contextual**
which come from different contexts
creates a tension and sets up a question.
What are these things doing together ?
They don't belong.

Because they don't belong
we look closely
we notice, we hear, we see
we question.
We may also be surprised or annoyed or amused.
Contra-contextual methods
encourage the spectator to re-evaluate his value system.

What about a piece of ballet with a pop sound score,
a Chopin Prelude with a rough and tumble throw and catch duo,
Classical Indian dancing with a Purcell score ?
Do I value the ballet scene or the pop scene ?
Am I a romantic at heart ?
Do I appreciate an aggressive, competitive attitude to life ?
Do I believe that cultural barriers should remain
or should be opened up?

Counterpointing music with movement                                           **counterpoint**
is primarily a matter of rhythm and phrasing.
The aim is to create a relationship
so that some sort of depth of texture is achieved
through a third statement of some sort.
Movement, music and movement/music are layers using
devices like anticipation of sound pattern by movement pattern,
repetition in the music but not in the movement,
contrast of pitch and level, of size and amplitude,
reiteration of movement material where none is in the music.
These are devices that can all be combined.
It is a way of adding a layer of fun,
of mystery, of play, of density, of contradiction.

Slavishly following the rhythmic beat of the music                            **mickey mousing**
accent for accent, phrase for phrase
is referred to as Mickey Mousing.
It can result in redundancy.
What the dance says
has already been heard in the music.
It can have a purpose when used sparingly
for it is a way of reinforcing an aural statement visibly
or a kinetic statement aurally.

It may be a means for comedy.
Combined with counterpoint
Mickey Mousing can add to the texture.

Another kind of Mickey Mousing
can also function
where the music has a verbal layer.
The words can be reflected in gestural choices.
"Hat" finds a heady gesture,
"Hit" finds an energetic fist
"Hot" finds a cooling down fan.
On an abstract level the rhythm is continuously overstated
while on an image level a second layer of meaning is offered.
Mark Morris makes it work
virtuosically.

Jiri Kylian's musicality is well known.
In **Svadebka (or Les Noces)**
to Stravinsky's score
his close visualisation of the rhythms of the music are a feature.
Although his movement invention and sense of design
are quite independent
his rhythms are not.
For some spectators they are too close to the Stravinsky
for comfort,
too dependent.

In **Sinfonietta** he is also very close to the Janáček score
for entrances, for phrasing, for dynamics,
for accents, for mood.
No co-existence for Kylian but integration.

In **Kaguyahime** he has a very different score to deal with.
Maki Isha's arhythmic soundscape
gives Kylian less possibility for visualisation.
His own inventive movement stands out.
He creates independently using the sound as atmosphere.
Or almost.
His penchant for Mickey Mousing creeps in
from time to time.

**tying in**

Less rigorous attachment of movement and sound
is possible in works where the elements are uncountable.
Electro-acoustic music
or non metric sound scores,
with breath rhythmed movement
or semi-improvised material
can tie in from time to time,
giving an overall impression

of two distinct but supportive elements.
Finding the cues is the challenge for the choreographer,
recognising the moments
is the challenge for the performer.

Unexpected sounds,                                                **chance**
unexpected interface
are what chance methods can produce.
There has to be a purpose in such a choice
to avoid it sounding like an amateur cacophony.
Choice within a carefully selected range of options
is a positive compromise.

After a work is almost completed choreographically            **framing**
it may need a frame,
an aural frame,
as a picture needs a visual one,
to set it apart from the noise world around it,
to give it the atmosphere the choreographer wants.
Sound helps the work to communicate
its feeling content.

Many a dance has been created and rehearsed to one piece of music,   **changing**
then changed for the production.
Whatever the reasons for abandoning a sound score -
it is too long,
it gives the wrong mood,
it is too fast, it is too well known,
someone else has used the same score -
waiting until the last moment
has proved traumatic
but successful.
Some choreographers always work that way
wanting the inspiration and constraints of music
to start and discipline their work,
while all along searching
for other possibilities for the final sound.

Rehearsing a piece without its music
is worth while.
It enables you to see what is securely there in the movement.
Dancers have to be able to hold their material's timing
and dynamic
whatever the sound.

**reading**

**Katherine Teck**
Ear Training for the Body : A dancer's guide to music (1994)

Teck gives a comprehensive guide written as a musician.

**Valerie Preston-Dunlop**
Dance Words (Chapter : The Sound and the Movement) (1995)

Both choreographers and musicians put their point of view on the function of sound in a dance and on their valued collaborative methods.

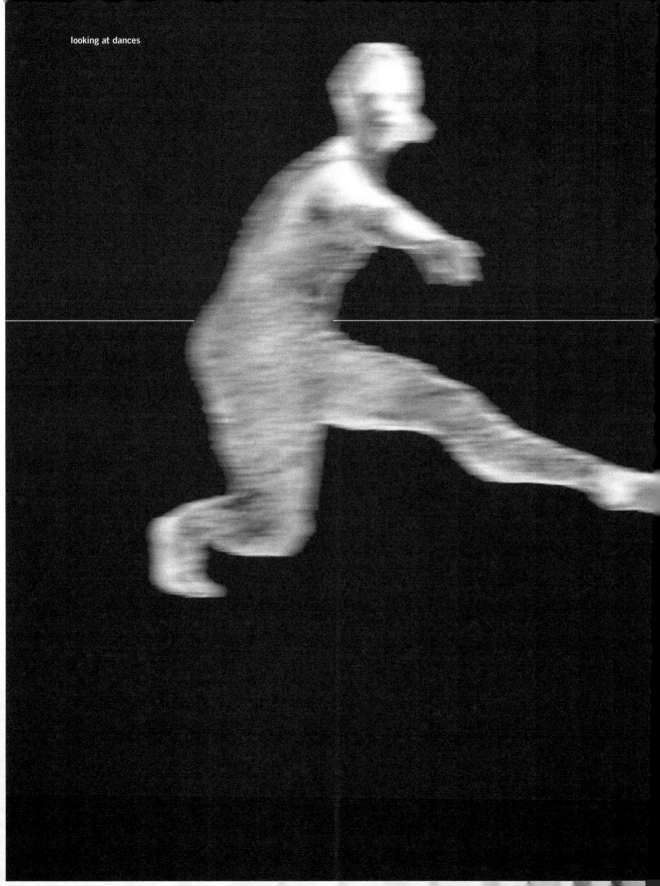

looking at dances

# movement
## space nexus

# a place for a dance
does where you dance matter ?

One dance can seem quite good in a studio,
looked at close to.
Put it on stage and it appears lost.
Equally a dance can feel like a study
until it is given breath by its right space.
Anticipating the space of the performance,
choosing one that will enhance the work
is essential.
Space speaks.

Presenting a work in a procenium theatre
with a clear divide between auditorium and stage
sets up the expectation of an illusionary world,
a magical world,
removed from the humdrum of the mundane.
That is what a procenium does.
That is how spectators will respond.
You need that divide, that distance,
for fairy tales,
for dance-dramas,
to help the spectator to share the magic.

**procenium theatre**

You can transgress the rules
as Bausch did in **Kontakthof**
by bringing her dancers down from the stage
walking them in and out of the seated spectators
offering them cups of tea.
The audience had no idea how to respond.

They squirmed in their seats,
not knowing where to look.
She made her point by allowing her use of space to speak for her.
This production was clearly something requiring attention.

Spaces have their unstated rules
which can help you if you use them
or purposefully subvert them.
They will hinder you
if you ignore their power.

**studio theatre**

Theatres with an informal divide between
those who do and those who watch
are difficult to use for illusion.
There is no architecture to inform you.
A degree of understanding between artist and appreciator
is unstated.
The limitations of the venue are accepted.
To behave in that space as if it were a procenium space
is to ask too much of it.

**in the round**

Having spectators all around
makes spatial difficulties and opportunities.
Where is front ?
Dancers easily become disoriented.
Centre becomes a special place.
How do you get on and off ?
A dancer's back has to be as interesting as any other side.
Counterpoint methods, layering devices,
need a fresh eye.
Illusion is impossible.
Why is "in the round" the choice for the work ?
Trying to adapt a piece made for a traditional fronted space
for performance in the round
is challenging for all.

**site specific**

Some works are made for a particular site.
They cannot be performed in any other place.
The movement arises out of the interface
between moving people and that special space.
Each site brings with it its own life.

If you choose an art gallery as a site for dance
you will bring with that choice
the behaviour that goes with looking at pictures.
Rosemary Butcher did with **Touch the Earth**
in the Whitechapel Art Gallery.
A gallery is not a site to sit in for the duration of the dance
but one in which to look

for as long or short a time as your interest suggests.
You can just pop in and out if you so wish.
The site has an aesthetic value of its own.
When the dance is over the gallery and its value are unchanged.

Dances in sites that are derelict
juxtapose the forgotten and the abandoned
with the cared for, possibly with the beautiful.
The nexus of site and movement constructs the message.

If you choose a public walkway
it will bring with it the public.
They will walk in their space,
possibly passing through the work
becoming for a while performers.
If the choreographer wants to merge with a mundane space
then choice of clothing is crucial.
There is nothing more out of place
than spangles in a park
unless they serve a purpose.
Street clothes might do it.

**public spaces**

Working in a public place
may require you to set up imaginary boundaries.
If you do not want the public to treat the space in its customary way
you have to let them know, somehow.
  They may see you as a trespasser
  and treat you so.
  The sheep did in Michèle Anne de Mey's **Love Sonnets.**

  She transformed her stage work **Sonatas 555**
  to **Love Sonnets,** a site specific version.
  The location is a rugged hillside,
  complete with shepherd and flock.
  The terrain is pebbled, then dusty sand,
  then a shingled slope.
  In it and on it they run, they throw themselves,
  they roll, they dance.
  The mix of mundane space with constructed dance material
  asks the question :
  Why dance here ?
  Is dance a theatre art ?
  Is running on pebbles dancing ?
  Is a hillside a dance space ?

  It provokes the question :
  Why not ?

Entry and exit of dancers in a public place can be a problem.
At what point do they cease to be public
and become performer ?
Having them hiding somewhere, behind a bush,
ready to emerge
is no solution.
Appearing in the distance, in a bunch,
gathering gradually from all sides,
can set up the event.
Having performers dressed in street clothes
(ostensibly the public),
becoming a performer with one step into the arena,
returning to be public from time to time,
asks :
Are dancers special or ordinary ?
Could I perform too ?

**ritual spaces**

Churches, temples, cathedrals,
are used for dances with a celebratory theme
or a ritual purpose.
The space suggests that, traditionally,
spectators are more than outsiders looking in.
They are members of that space
sharing a common belief.
A secular work in such a space would be contra-contextual
thereby setting its own agenda.
Are sacred spaces sacred any more ?
Can the secular and the sacred intermingle ?
Is art as much the domain of the soul as religion ?

Entrances and exits,
costumes,
set various expectations in place.
A procession introduces ritual.
Emergence from the congregation encourages participation.
Professional, highly trained dancers set one scene.
Ordinary men and women as performers set another.
Choice is all.

**video dance**

Many dances that we see are on video, not live.
Some are video dances
made especially for that mixed media
in which video space is an element from the beginning.
Shot, distance, angle, fade, cut,
are elements to use.
They shift the phenomenon of living in a continuous body
for the body can be cut up.
It can disappear and re-appear.
It can be overlaid with other bodies.

The camera can jump time, it can jump place.

There are stage works put on video
in which one space is given up for another.
  Forsythe comments that
  **Love Songs**, on stage, is more abstract than
  **Love Songs** on film.
  The proximity of viewer to performer
  made possible by camera shot
  adds a voyeuristic element.
  The distress of an ended relationship is thrust upon
  the spectator.

It is just not possible to capture a dance on screen.
The result is a changed work.
The audience's eye is dictated to by the camera.
You can no longer linger on what you want to see.
The camera looks for you.
Close ups change your perception.
Form is subverted, drama is heightened.

reading

**Gaston Bachelard**
The Poetics of Space (1969)

In this classic paperback Bachelard writes of spaces in general. His point is that a space is never meaningless. Each one carries its own signification.

**Miranda Tufnell and Chris Crickmay**
Body Space Image: Notes Towards Improvisation and Performance (1993)

Tufnell writes as a performer with an interest in the interaction of movement and spaces.

**David Allen and Stephanie Jordan**
(eds.) Parallel Lines: Media Representations of Dance (1992)

Articles on dance and the media address the issue of video and film spaces, what they contain and how they influence the dance and the dancer.

**Valerie Preston-Dunlop**
Dance Words (Chapter : The Dance Space) (1995)

# transforming the space
## how do designers design a dance ?

The space that a dance will occupy
is transformed into a fictional place
by the design elements.

A space is always designed.                                    **primary decisions**
Leaving a space in its natural condition
is a design decision.

The first thing it has to become is
a place for dancers to be in,
a place where what they do can be seen to advantage.
Clutter clutters.
A black box encloses.
A cyclorama opens up.
A view of backstage workings
sets a functional environment.

What is put into the space                                     **decor**
particularises it.
It becomes a place.
It can become an emotional landscape
through setting up metaphors by simple means -
one old chair, one abstract form, one rope.

It can become a domestic scenario -
cosy, if things are as they should be,
topsy turvy if a sofa is on its side.

Slides on a cloth or a white wall
transform the space to wherever the image suggests.
Contra-contextual elements pose the question :
where are we ?

Breaking up the space
with rostra, with boxes,
with hanging pillars, with balloons, with falling petals,
adds a complexity for the viewer
which will confuse or explain,
but at any rate offers interest.

> Kristina de Chatel breaks up the space in **Paletta**
> with three transparent columns
> in each of which is a dancer.
> In so doing she creates two kinds of space
> for two kinds of choreography,
> one for dancers rooted to the spot
> but free to use the transparent walls for off-balance supports,
> the other for dancers free to travel past and around the columns
> but limited by the pull of gravity.

**lighting**

Lighting also sets an emotional temperature,
creates virtual architecture,
divides the space into separate domains.

While lighting may create an agenda of its own
it must primarily light dancers.
Low level side light can sculpt the body,
back light can silhouette a figure.
Focusing on one dancer, on one spot, prioritizes.
Field lighting does the opposite.
It lights equally all dancers and all parts of the place.
It avoids priviledge.
It democratises the space.

> In **Swan Song** Christopher Bruce uses a chair in a dark place
> with a high window through which a light shafts down.
> He conjures a place, a cell, a prison
> with these simple means.
> Each element of the decor is a metaphor.
> The chair is a safe haven
> which the prisoner is denied,
> with which he is tormented.
> The window is an unobtainable freedom.
> The light is the longing of his spirit,
> the route of his ultimate journey.

The set can function as a frame to a finished dance.                          **framing**
It completes it, gives it a layer.
This is the traditional way, the simplest way.
It completes the classic process.
Find your music, cast your dancers, make your movement.
Produce it by costuming it, staging it, lighting it.

Some choreographers prefer to interact.                          **interactional space**
The set is there from the beginning -
the dancers move in it, on it, around it, through it.
The dance does not exist without it.
The meaning is not in the movement per se.
It is in interactional movement, there, with that, in that.

    This is just what Suzy Blok and Christopher Steel do in **Still You.**
    The table between them is both an interactional set
    and a metaphor of an emotional barrier.
    They dance in and around and under the table
    with no sound but their own.
    It is violent play
    given all manner of gradations by their interaction with the set.

Water may be included.
It is a place to drown in, to wade in, to float in, to wash in.
    Water begins and ends Edward Lock's **La La La Duo One**
    which is otherwise an athletic two-some on dry land.
    It offers an opening image of fish out of water.
    Does that influence how we read the dance ?
    I think it does.
At the end the dancers swim away
so the spectator is probably confounded.

Rubbish may be included as something to kick around,
soil on the ground to get mudded in,
autumn leaves to shuffle in,
grass to loll on,
park seats to meet on,
swings to swing on.........

The set may be kinetic -
trickling sand, dripping water,
a device much used in Butoh productions.
Things lifting and lowering, things swung,
things thrown on stage,
smoke screens, coloured puffs.........
all kinetic.

Secondary action accompanying the stage action
through simultaneous playing of a TV programme,

a prepared video, a computer game, a film,
provide a foil with which the main action interacts.
All these possibilities serve their purpose
or turn into gimmicks.

Each one adds its own layer of meaning
as well as being worth watching in its own right.
Each one needs to contribute to a metaphor.
What the metaphor refers to is a matter for the choreographer
and the designer.

**reading**

### Ana Sanchez-Colberg
"You can see it like this or like that"
in ~ Allen and Jordan (eds) Parallel Lines : Media Representations of Dance (1992)

Sanchez-Colberg's article focuses on Bausch and her contracontextual use of the nexus between the body and specific settings which Bausch achieves by creating environments which undermine expected meanings through paradox.

### David Buckland
"Designing Motion in Dance" in Dance Theatre Journal Vol 12  No4 (1996)

### Peter Mumford
"Lighting Dance" in Dance Research Vol 3 No 2 (1985)

Buckland and Mumford are both acclaimed designers for dance.

### Francis Reid
Lighting the Stage (1995)

# conclusion

# putting it all together
## making use of communication theory, semiotics, the nexus of the dance in dance making, in dancing and in spectating

The choreological way of looking at things
from several points of view,
the makers', the dancers', the viewers',
has been central to this text
in the content and the organisation of the separate discussions.

In the dance itself they all happen together.
That is what makes it so absorbing.
In an attempt to see how it all works together
here are several choreographies
at different stages of readiness.

While looking, the communicative functions will be in mind -
the referential, the metalinguistic, the performative,
the aesthetic, the phatic, and the injunctive.
So too will the four strands of the medium,
the performer, the movement, the sound, the space,
and their nexus,
integrated, co-existent, contra-contextual et al.
The poietic signs, those in the trace
and the esthesic level added by the viewer
will be remembered.

If these choreological choices are worth their salt
they should help us to see how Ed Wubbe
with Scapino Rotterdam,
make their production function
with their co-operating team Pamela Horoet for decor,
Bruno Veen for light,
with music by Godflesh and Stern.

**Ed Wubbe's *Kathleen***

The work is established from the beginning
as an accessible piece
within the genre of Belgium / Dutch modernity.
Wubbe establishes that across all the strands of the dance medium.

The dancers are dressed in functional clothing
connoting current daily wear.
Nothing ornamental is offered,
nothing in the set, the clothing, the hair styles, the sound.
Through an integration of the strands
we are offered a metaphor for current street culture.

In terms of codes
if we have seen Vandekeybus and de Keesmaeker
we can unlock the code.
If we know Robbins' *West Side Story*
we can locate the history of the street dance concept.

With a wide experience of choreography over the past twenty years,
viewers can see influences from other choreographers -
Bausch for example from her use of children's games.
Other choreographers have used casual observation
by the rest of the cast during solos and duets.
One has heard interrupted and repeated text fragments before.
Recognition of influence does not detract from Wubbe's work.
Such poietic knowledge serves to locate him.
What we will want to know is
how Ed Wubbe will handle the codes.

We see that he puts his stamp on it quite early on.
Wubbe can create original movement material
which we see the women dancing.
He admires articulation.
He likes structuring devices.
Reiteration, canon, variation hold the work together.
He enjoys dynamic variation, stark dynamic range.
Already the recognition of place, time and culture are clear
and dealt with poetically in the movement.

The performative function is working
for we see the commitment of the dancers,
we have utter confidence in their technical prowess,
we see them as empowered individuals.

Exactly who the Kathleen of the title is we do not know.
The set proclaims that she has "a big cunt".
She is one of the women dancers
with no strong distinguishing marks.
If the title refers to someone else,

someone we are expected to have heard of,
a particular Kathleen in the news,
then we are not let into that knowledge.

Early on juxtapositioning is presented
as a method of narrating relationship.
Two forms of sound overlap that do not match.
Men and women meet, compete and confront.

Wubbe's aesthetic taste is made known
by his choice of sound, clothing, decor
and of movement material.
Glamour is eschewed but not virtuosity.
Macho maleness is enjoyed.
Brawn is honoured in both sexes.

Occasional fleeting denotive signs are given in the movement
and the clothing.
Sexual gestures, aggressive focus, quotations from clubbing,
leather, knuckle-dusters, skateboarding, drug abuse flash by.
Hyped step patterns by the women, gender solidarity,
contrast with male competitiveness, male hesitation and doubt.
Mutual partner exchange sets the scene of sexual indulgence.

Wubbe is not going to over-describe.
His message on the wall directs our eye.
It does more than suggest
yet he allows us to meet him with our own imagination
and experience.
He does not ask us to sit back and watch a narrative
but he does ask us to recognise
the dominant role of sex in current culture.

He uses text to home us in
to the tough competitive culture
of a post-modern environment.
The repetition of short verbal phrases
suggests one man's view of the narrative :
"It was a conscious decision on my part.........power......".

Having set the scene
Wubbe enters the most difficult part of choreography.
He sets himself to develop and articulate what he has already set up
rather thant move on in a narrative
which is a much easier option.
This is where the spectator might think :
"This has gone on long enough."
This is where he has to hold the audience's interest.
He does it by several means -

shifting the dynamic of the work,
agitation, manic energy level, more off balance falling,
more confrontational encounters,
more sexual power games,
interspersed with glimpses of tenderness,
of exhaustion and reluctance.
He does it through his inventiveness of solo material,
by the brevity of duos,
by the variety of ensemble, solo, trio episodes
by sheer virtuosic dancing.
He may be seen as nearly overdoing the borrowing from the Belgians
and yet the moves always have his signature.

Wubbe comes to the ultimate difficulty of how to end a dance.
Rather surprisingly he stops being episodic.
Instead he narrates.
The surprise is through the shift of codes.
This woman must be Kathleen, for she is named in the title.
Instead of an archetype she becomes an individual persona, a role.
We learn from her movement that she has had enough,
she is collapsing.
Just what has caused her demise now, at this point,
we are not told but we wonder.
We learn from his almost straight behavioural references
that one man cares,
reinforced by the denotive crashes on the piano.
Does his world crash around him ?
We don't know.

Why shouldn't Wubbe shift code ?
He can.
The problem is that he has set up so consistently
a method of integrated strands, archetypal personas, episodic structure.
He then changes gear to present us with Kathleen
to show us his attitude to the topic.
But not clearly enough.
We need more
to be able to share with her as a particluar young woman.

Why shouldn't he end with an unresolved point ?
Valid question.
Some dances do, successfully.
The questions he leaves us with here are particular.
It is universal questions left open that start people talking.
Here we are bothered by lack of personal information
on a woman we know almost nothing about as an individual
except her sexual availability.
That insignificant query looms far larger
than the main plot of the work

which is substantial and worth dwelling on.

Each of us will have our own response to **Kathleen**
adding an esthesic layer of meanings.
For me the ending is unsatisfactory
while the dance as a whole communicates significantly
and outstandingly.
But I am only one spectator.

We look at Anderson at the beginning stages of her new work
for her male company, the Featherstonehaughs,
six male dancers with pronounced individuality.
As I watch her working
her concentration is on setting up her self imposed rules
within which she will make original material.

Already her research for sources is done.
She will focus on the drawings and paintings of Egon Schiele,
the Viennese Secessionist artist
who shocked the public
in the first decade of the twentieth century
with his contorted nudes.
The piece will become
"an engrossing journey into Schiele's world."

She sets about making the first strings.
Her knowledge of her sources is detailed,
her use of them is meticulous,
down to the last finger nail,
the last eye gesture.
She works on transposing a drawing into a physical act,
on getting into and out of each pose
in such a way that noone could foresee the coming position.
Each connection is closely worked.
Sometimes two dancers must keep close,
wrapping round each other, knotting and unknotting,
until a solution is found satisfactory to her eye.
She works unhurriedly, concentrated, collaboratively.

She wants some familiarity for the spectator
which she then disrupts
to create unfamiliar moments,
weird, bizarre, as Schiele is.
Her movements have no name,
they are unclassifiable.
Bizarre is not only a quality of Schiele.
It is a well established quality of Anderson
presented by her two companies, these male dancers
and the female company The Cholmondeleys.

At another time the movement's quality is what she controls.
"Not incident, incident, incident -
more chewy, spongey."
Exact rhythmic nuance is agreed,
"and-six wasn't it, not six-and ?"
as the men grapple with the bizarre angularity,
the detail and the syncopation.
Metric rhythm precision and unexpectedness
are the hall marks of Anderson's phrasing.
"I wouldn't have put it on the beat, surely?"

Anderson focuses on generating motion.
Only then does she ascribe motivation
to enable the dancers to intend the same detail
on each performance.
"You're taking your jumper off here" -
"You're barring his way" -
"You pull then let go."
The movement is not about taking a jumper off.
It is about Schiele's nude drawing.
Struggling out of a tight jumper
is what one incident might feel like to a dancer dancing it.

Anderson misses nothing,
looks at each image from several viewpoints,
anticipating how she might eventually use it.
Everything she wants to be seen is worked
according to the parameters she is crystalising.
Any move which the dancer says must happen
for technical reasons
but goes against her eye
should be hidden.
"Hide that strength."
"How you got there must be invisible".

Nothing is structured yet,
just material, material, material,
in strings.
Each section of the work is allotted its own set of limitations
around the common theme of Schiele's angular and erotic
imagination,
seen through Anderson's eye.

The communicative functions uppermost in her eye
are the injunctive
and the metalinguistic.
The audience need to feel a bit odd, uncomfortable,
Schiele is odd and uncomfortable.
The audience will become voyeurs.

Anderson never flags up incidents to prepare the specator's eye.
Each image emerges via an unforeseen route.

At this stage
the movement and the performer are the strands that she uses.
One physique against another,
one dynamic colouring against another,
one dancer's idiosyncracy against another's.
Sound is irrelevant as yet.
Although she knows full well what it will be
her ear does not inspire Anderson, Schiele does.
Use of the stage space, the design of it, is yet to come.
This piece is not interactional with a set
as some of Anderson's have been.

What she does in these early stages is
discover her own web of limitations
working on them until they become the codes of the piece.
Eventually what will take the stage is a fifty minute work :
**"The Featherstonehaugh's Draw on the Sketchbooks of Egon Schiele."**

As a jury member on a international choreographic festival
directed to give a practical **relecture** after the performance
I found myself with a quartet.
The work was highly commended by the jury as a whole
for its crafting and movement invention.

**a quartet for a festival**

Were crafting and invention enough to win acclaim ?
No, but they were substantially impressive.
What was missing ?
The problem lay in the apparent lack of motivation
for the innovations.
If you are going to break movement codes
(which is what she did)
then that iconoclasm needs to serve some purpose.
Hers seemed to be perversity for its own sake.
No other rules were broken.
The sound was unmemorable.
The costuming was conformist.
So what were we to think or feel or enjoy or question ?

In semiotic terms
the metalinguistic function was functioning exquisitely
but unsupported by anything else.
The exacerbating problem lay in the performers.
They were not up to offering anything beyond
a plain rendering of the movement.
They were not able to give a performative dimension to the work.
If they had been one might have been able to say

this new language, danced with articulation and dextrous intention,
is worth looking at in its own right.
The aesthetic function could then have worked for her.
She could have given more thought to the costuming
so that her dancers' look, their physique and colouring,
worked for her aesthetically rather than functionally.

Alternatively she could have brainstormed her own motives
to get out what was leading her to break the movement codes.
What message was that hiding ?
What values did she want to test ?
Then she could give her credo to her dancers
for their look, their intention, their costuming.
The invention's perversity might become accessible.

**a piece for teenagers**

This work was presented for a **relecture**
prior to entering for selection for a festival.
It was a concise dance some five minutes long
for a group of able amateur young dancers.
It had a narrative theme without telling a story.

The dancers were birds.
The stage was turned into a place
through economical use of poles
through which the dancers passed
and in which they rested.

It was a well structured dance.
It used the space purposefully and with interesting patterns.
The movement material was referential, almost,
bird-like without depicting.

Costume was adequate within a budget.
Sound was appropriate without dominating.
Should we just accept that it was a competent piece ?
Could it be more ?

The choreographer had allowed herself
to be dominated rhythmically by counting.
The dancers rose and fell, made patterns and stood still,
to what one knew were unspoken counts.
The dancers complied.
They were objects not birds.

Birds are alive.
Allowing the counts to fade into the background
we asked the dancers to breathe their movement
to find the breath rhythm inherent in it.
They did and the movement came to life.

They took charge of their material.
They started to sense it rather than do it.
A clearer intention emerged
an image of flight, of wings, was apparent.

As they began to take control of their own rhythmic phrasing
the regiment of birds became untidy.
Did the choreographer want uniformity ?
All the time ?
There is something magical about the unison flight of a flock
but on the ground, too ?
Because it had been counts that held the group together
now that the counts had receded
the dancers had to find another way to unite.
They needed to sense each other,
to use their lateral vision of each other,
to listen for the slight breath sounds.
To do this they had to take control even more
of their own movement.
They had to feel their responsibility as performers
so that we could believe in them.
They could and we did.

The music / movement correlation got slightly out of synchrony.
Did that matter ?
The choreographer had thought it would
but it did not.
It gave a sense of independence to the flock as a whole.
It hid from the spectator
the craft of the movement / music structuring.

Perhaps the choreographer had underestimated her dancers.
Perhaps she had been wary of letting go her control.
She had made the trace
but she did not quite know how to empower her performers.
Movement does not speak.
Intending performers do.

This ensemble work was ambitious.                              **ensemble piece**
A twenty minute group piece for four women and two men.
It was of high standard, interesting on the whole
but with dead patches.

It suffered from the common complaint of taped music dominance.
The invention had started from the sound.
The dance had then found its own life, its own sequencing,
but the fixed score on tape could not adjust.
Something had to be done.

We danced the dance without music.
Almost immediately
movement padding inserted to fit in with the sound lengths
became apparent.
It stuck out like a sore thumb.
Why are you doing that ?
How does it follow from this ?
The padding was removed
to reveal a much more focused, tight work.
But it had no sound.

The temptation to cut the music was acute.
It was resisted.
We tried the same dance with a score that was not metric,
that had a comparable mood.
The music had pauses in it that could be shortened
or lengthened.
The dancers found that they could free up their phrasing,
could speed up and slow down
to enhance the intention of the piece.
What had been a counted construction to Arvo Pärt
became a phenomenal work with Takemitsu.

**a work in progress**

A young choreographer has a work in progress
which has been tried out in several low key venues.
Here are some of the discussions that took place
as she edited the work.

The event is for two men and two women dancers,
three musicians, a text, a film, lighting.
This is a border crossing piece of some seventy minutes.
She has a track record of interesting low-funded theatre pieces.
At present she is searching to expand her way of working.

Early on one male dancer speaks.
He recites a monologue on aspiration and futility.
It is excellently spoken as he dances.
The performative is functioning well through him.
The words inform us and can please poetically.

The second man dances a solo.
It is crucially placed at the beginning of the work.
He is interesting to look at,
quite distinct and individual.
His performance of what he has to do is adequate,
but not strong enough to engage us aesthetically.
The aesthetic and performative values are not strong enough.
Because the material is competent without being rivetting
we need to look at what he is offering for its reference value

otherwise we cannot become involved.

The purpose of his material is fuzzy.
What does this early scene setting solo offer ?
What should a spectator know by the end of it ?
How should a spectator be looking at the work
by the end of the solo ?
We either have to be satisfied with it for its own sake
or because we understand what he is refering to,
or because the material is innovative,
or because his performance is compelling.

The choreographer wanted us to understand
but her idea had remained private.
She had not embodied it in the trace
in a way that could be retrieved by a spectator.
Indeed what she was asking movement to convey was beyond it.
She will need to focus her desired image,
to hone down the material
to say just what is needed.

The piece opens with a tableau of four individuals
distanced from each other,
who are organised geometrically.
It is an aesthetically pleasing image.
That sets up an expectation for a formal ingredient to the work
but the geometry never re-occurs
either in repetition or variation.
Is this a wasted opportunity ?
Could it serve as a structuring method
for linking the episodes of the work ?
Could it have a strong phatic function through this means?

She tried it, and was satisfied
with the increased sense of architectural form that emerged.

How we look at the movement alongside the film section
was determined inevitably by the references in the film.
Film extracts almost always dictate.

The correlation of these visual images with the movement
had been difficult to achieve
because the film did not arrive until near the performance date.
The film maker had ideas of his own,
the film maker could not see the finished dance,
nor could the choreographer finish until she had seen the film.

The result was that the film served little purpose.
It appeared almost to be a gimmick

rather than an integral part of the work.
Because the choreographer was using integration
as the nexus between the strands
preparation time to achieve integration had been essential.
It had not been scheduled adequately.

The idea of visual images to cue the spectator was admirable.
Not through this film.
Through another ? Through slides ?

The sound was layered.
The occasional text, the composition for live piano,
the inventive drumming, the gutteral vocalisation, came in and out
from different parts of the performance area and auditorium.
The movement and sound rhythms were independent,
tying in quite carefully with no Mickey Mousing.

As the piece progressed
the pianist/composer became a dancer.
So too did the vocal improvisor.
The change of role intrigued.
It border crossed.
They both performed well.
Both were visually compelling, too.
The drummer took the stage later
with a huge sabre
which he swung almost ceremoniously.

The choreographer had wanted to bring in a flavour of ritual.
Hence the ceremonial gestures.
Why she wanted to was unclear.
To do what ?
Why shift the work in that direction ?
Should there be a ritual flavour throughout ?
Possibly she was enticed into including the sabre
because the drummer was a martial artist.
Either way it was back to the studio
to reinforce, to cut.

All the border crossing was, in the main, worth looking at.
The aesthetic, the performative, the metalinguistic
were functioning.
What it meant did not seem to matter.
One section on partnerships
drew heavily on Belgian throw and catch material,
not entirely derivatively
but enough for anyone to recognise
and ask why.
When throw-and-catch was first introduced

it worked because it was new.
Then it became more daring, and worked because of that.
Then what ?
How to mark that material with her own stamp for her own purpose
was the choreographer's dilemma.
It needed more work.
She had to ask herself :
"Why am I doing this ?
What catch, which throw, to function how for the spectator ?"

In another section of the piece
the meaning was clear.
The women circled round the men
who were engaged with each other in an encounter.
In the context of the piece as a whole
one could read what she wanted us to see.
Beyond the meaning there was not much else.
Can refering be enough to hold the spectator ?
Probably not.

How could the circling hold our eye ?
Rhythmical sharpening, more focussed intention,
more demanding material,
a purposeful re-iteration of earlier material ?
Back to the studio to try it out.

This promising work is still in progress.
It is shaping up through a clearer vision of what is needed
to communicate what the choreographer intended.
A more focused use of the semiotic functions available to her
is becoming, gradually, part of her choreographic process.
"It takes.......................................................time."

Matthew Bourne's reworking of the three act **Cinderella**
ran for a season at the Piccadilly Theatre in London's West End.
It displays an array of sources.
He has retained the original Prokofiev score in tact.
He holds to
the dysfunctional family members of the traditional story -
the incapable father, the wicked step-mother,
the ugly step-sisters plus ugly brothers,
and Cinders.
Here the conventions of the fairy story cease
for his heroic figure is not a prince but a World War Two pilot.
His fairy godmother is a male guardian angel.

The context is war-torn London in The Blitz of 1940.
There is no sign of a sumptuous palace
nor a kitchen floor to be scrubbed.

**Matthew Bourne's**
*Cinderella*

Cinders' task is more up to date -
to stay in and look after father,
disabled, geriatric, housebound in a wheel chair.
Bourne gives no magic pumpkin transforming to a carriage
but a shiny white motor bike and sidecar instead.

Reference to the war is aural through the stereo roar
of aircraft overhead,
explosions and sirens interspersed with Prokofiev.
Reference is visual through the 1940's civvy street costumes,
the forces' uniforms, the Air Raid Wardens' tin hats
and the obligatory gas masks.
The set refers variously to the vaults of the London Underground,
the moveable screens of a convalescent ward for war victims,
a dance hall, a family house, or streets in The Blackout.

The men of the ensemble are not aristocratic playboys
but brave men in the armed forces.
The women are multifarious Londoners, in uniform and out,
coping with the war,
dancing to keep their spirits up.

Bourne has to address layers of codes
anticipated by his theatre audience.
This **Cinderella** follows the company's all male **Swan Lake**
a long season sell out success.
Audience expectation will be high and directed.
Stepping on the familiarity of the classic Ashton ballet,
admired and loved by many, including Bourne,
could be treacherous ground.
The theatrical extravagance of 1990's musicals
**(Starlight Express, Les Mis., Miss Saigon.........)**
where mechanically rich sets preside
could be difficult to follow.
Mixing the movement modes
of ballet/contemporary/theatrical business/behaviour
could confuse.
The Prokofiev score carries an aura of high art
while Bourne offers a broader palette.
With this history to the work
spectator expectations could be a hazard.
That is at the heart of Bourne's decision making.

**Cinderella** is produced by and with AMP
Bourne's company Adventures in Motion Pictures.
He values collaborative working methods
with skilled artists across all the strands of the dance medium.
Communication is a priority.
Bourne's discussion of his work

is punctuated by "our audience."
He aims to satisfy not confuse.
He offers a rich and varied experience not an esoteric or elitist one.
He wants to surprise not shock,
to make them comfortable not discomforted.
Many return to see the work several times
knowing that it will contain enough complexity
for more than one looking.

In the balance between the six communicative functions
he prioritizes the referential over the aesthetic
while always wanting a poetic resonance.
He treads a fine line between theatre and dance.
To that end references abound.
A few remain private to him.
The central themes he wants to form clearly in the work's fabric.
Some he keeps open to interpretation and individual imagination.
"Basic clarity with a bit of mystery."

References to films are slipped in.
**Brief Encounter** can be recognised in the railway station scene.
**A Matter of Life and Death** pervaded his thinking
of Cinderella herself hanging between life and death in The Blitz,
as everyone did.
Characters are thought through,
their history created and shared in discussion,
written down by all casts.
Cinderella, for example, became a many-faceted person
centrally a frump with a second fantacy life explored in the work.
To help the audience understand that
signposts are offered,
her plain hairdo and make up, her spectacles,
her first duet with a dummy not a real man.
More are offered again, carefully, through each scene.

The performative function is crucial for Bourne.
The input from the company is continuously nurtured
through the season.
Each company member's self worth is valued.
They are not instruments for him
but co-authors and actors.
Notes after a performance continue throughout the run.
Complacency with a role is avoided.
The audience-performer relationship
is continually sought, experienced and responded to.

How to set up the communication and maintain it, not subvert it,
is deliberated.
To that end sounds and sights fill the auditorium

as spectators arrive.
The mood is set up in anticipation of the action itself.
Tensions in the narrative at the end of an act
to be resolved in the next
have to carry the audience through the intervals.
Bourne works to maintain their curiosity.

The preview period
with its performances prior to the critical appraisal by the press
is when Bourne's choreographic and theatrical eye work overtime.
The show as a whole is seen by him for the first time.
"I have to separate myself from the knowledge I have of the content."
He looks and asks himself and his friends :
"What did you see ?"
The revelation of images blurred,
stories not clear, surprises mistimed,
is anticipated by Bourne.
For **Cinderella** he completely re-worked the Prologue.
It was theatrically strong in itself
but out of place in the whole work,
too elaborate,
setting up expectations that were not dealt with in the later scenes.
The opening of the ballroom scene he tightened.
The initial pose of each figure was too decorous.
They needed to suggest dead bodies after an air raid.
Parts rehearsed in a smaller space did not work on stage in the set.
He had to start one event all over again.

Is there still editting to be done, after 90 performances ?
Yes, says Bourne.
Partly because his own imagination is still working on it,
he literally wants to try out new ideas.
Because he aims for a difficult concept
namely to present the events through the eyes of its main
character, Cinderella,
rather than contenting himself
with a simple narration of a fairy story,
the refinement needed to create the transitions from reality to dream
takes time to crystalise
and rehearsal time to formulate.

Bourne's eye is never closed.

# dance works cited

| | |
|---|---|
| **Lea Anderson** | Les Six Belles (1997)<br>Transitions Dance Company |
| | The Featherstonehaughs Draw on the<br>Sketches of Egon Schiele (1998)<br>Featherstonehaughs |
| **Frederick Ashton** | Symphonic Variations (1946)<br>Sadlers Wells Ballet |
| | Tales of Beatrix Potter (1970)<br>Royal Ballet |
| **George Balanchine** | Orpheus (1948)<br>Ballet Society (New York City Ballet) |
| **Pina Bausch** | Bluebeard (1977)<br>Wuppertal Tanztheater |
| | Café Müller (1978)<br>Wuppertal Tanztheater |
| | Kontakthof (1980)<br>Wuppertal Tanztheater |
| **Michael Bennet<br>and Bob Amon** | A Chorus Line (1994)<br>Broadway Musical |
| **David Bintley** | Still Life at the Penguin Café (1981)<br>The Royal Ballet |
| **Suzi Blok and<br>Christopher Steel** | Still You (1995)<br>Blok and Steel |

| Matthew Bourne | Swan Lake (1995) |
| | Adventures in Motion Pictures |
| | Cinderella (1997) |
| | Adventures in Motion Pictures |
| Trisha Brown | MO (1995) |
| | Trisha Brown Company |
| Claude Brumachon | Naufragés (1989) |
| | Transitions Dance Company |
| Christopher Bruce | Swan Song (1987) |
| | London Festival Ballet |
| Rosemary Butcher | Touch the Earth (1987) |
| | Rosemary Butcher Dance Company |
| Merce Cunningham | Torse (1976) |
| | Merce Cunningham Dance Company |
| | Beach Birds (1992) |
| | Merce Cunningham Dance Company |
| Kristina de Chatel | Paletta (1992) |
| | Kristina de Chatel Dance Group |
| Rudi van Dantzig | Monument for a Dead Youth (1962) |
| | Netherlands National Ballet |
| Siobhan Davies | White Man Sleeps (1988) |
| | Siobhan Davies Company |
| Ulysses Dove | Dancing on the Front Porch of Heaven (1992) |
| | Royal Swedish Ballet |
| | Vespers (1986) |
| | Alvin Ailey Company |
| Michael Flatley and traditional | Riverdance (1995) |
| | Riverdance Irish Dance Company |
| William Forsythe | Love Songs (1989) |
| | Joffrey Ballet, film version |
| | In the Middle Somewhat Elevated (1988) |
| | Paris Opera Ballet |
| Antonio Gadès | Blood Wedding (1981) |
| | Antonio Gades Company |

| | |
|---|---|
| **Itzik Galili** | When You See God Tell Him (1995)<br>Galili and Jennifer Hanna |
| **Martha Graham** | Appalachian Spring (1944)<br>Martha Graham Company<br><br>Diversion of Angels (1948)<br>Martha Graham Company<br><br>Primitive Mysteries (1931)<br>Martha Graham Company |
| **Doris Humphrey** | Day on Earth (1947)<br>Limòn Company |
| **Carlotta Ikeda** | Aï Amor (1993)<br>Ikeda and Ko Murobushi |
| **Shobana Jeyasingh** | Can They Tell Stories (1993)<br>Shobana Jeyasingh Company |
| **Kurt Jooss** | Green Table (1932)<br>Ballets Jooss |
| **Anna Theresa de Keersmaeker** | Achterland (1990)<br>Rosas |
| **Jiri Kyliàn** | Kaguyahime (1988)<br>Nederlands Danstheater<br><br>Obscure Temptations (1991)<br>Nederlands Danstheater 3<br><br>Sarabande (1990)<br>Nederlands Danstheater<br><br>Sinfonietta (1978)<br>Nederlands Danstheater<br><br>Svadebka (1982)<br>Nederlands Danstheater |
| **Leonid Mikhailovitch Lavrovsky** | Romeo and Juliet (1940)<br>Kirov |
| **Edward Lock** | Duo One (1993)<br>La La La Human Sex |
| **Gillian Lynne** | A Simple Man (1988)<br>Northern Ballet Theatre |
| **Kenneth Macmillan** | Romeo and Juliet (1965)<br>Royal Ballet, Prokofiev |

| | |
|---|---|
| **Gilles Maheu and**<br>**Danielle Tardif** | Le Dortoir (1989)<br>Theatergroep Carbonne 14 |
| **Hans van Manen** | Two (1990)<br>Nederlands Danstheater |
| **Victoria Marks** | Mothers and Daughters (1994)<br>Victoria Marks Performers |
| **Michèle Anne de Mey** | Love Sonnets (1994)<br>video adaptation of Sonata 555 |
| **Mark Morris** | Love Song Waltzes (1989)<br>Mark Morris Dance Company |
| **Lloyd Newson** | Strange Fish (1993)<br>DV8 Physical Theatre |
| **Bronislava Nijinska** | Les Noces (1923)<br>Ballets Russes |
| **Stephen Petronio** | Middlesex Gorge (1993)<br>Stephen Petrnio Company |
| **Ton Simons** | In the Studio (Shapes) (1995) |
| **Twyla Tharp** | Push comes to shove (1976)<br>American Ballet Theatre |
| **Hans Tuerlings** | A Noeud Couland (1989)<br>Reflex / Dansgezelschap |
| **Anthony Tudor** | Romeo and Juliet (1943)<br>American Ballet Theater |
| **Wim Vandekeybus** | La Mentira (1990)<br>Ultima Vez<br><br>Roseland (1990)<br>Wim Wandekeybus Company |
| **Ed Wubbe** | Kathleen (1994)<br>Scapino Ballet |

# suggested reading

| | |
|---|---|
| **Adshead, J.** | ed. Choreography Principles and Practice (1987)<br>Guildford, National Resource Centre for Dance |
| **Allen, D.**<br>**and Jordan, S.** | Parallel Lines: Media Representations<br>of Dance (1992)<br>London, Arts Council Publications |
| **Argyle, M.** | The Psychology of Interpersonal<br>Behaviour (1967)<br>Harmsworth, Penguin |
| **Armelagos, A.**<br>**and Sirridge, M.**<br>**Bachelard G.** | "The Identity Crisis in Dance"<br>Journal of Aesthetics and Art Criticism (1978)<br>(ed) The Poetics of Space (1994)<br>New York, Orion Press |
| **Banes, S.** | Writing Dancing in the Age of<br>Post Modernism (1994)<br>Hanover, University of New England<br><br>Terpsichore in Skeakers (1980)<br>Boston, Houghton, Mifflin |
| **Blom, L.A.**<br>**and Chaplin, L.T.** | The Intimate Act of Choreography (1982)<br>Pittsburgh, University of Pittsburg<br><br>The Moment of Movement (1988)<br>London, Dance Books |

Buckland, D.    "Design in Motion" (1996)
in Dance Theatre Journal, Vol 12 No 4.

Cunningham, M    The Dancer and the Dance (1991)
and Leschaeve, J.    New York Marion Boyes

Field, D    The Study of Education in the Arts (1973)
and Newick, J.    London, Routledge Kegan Paul

Fiske, J.    Introduction to Communication Studies (1990)
London, Routledge

Foster, S.L.    Reading Dance (1986)
Berkeley, University of California Press

Corporealities: Dancing Knowledge
Culture and Power (1995)
London, Routledge

Fraleigh, S.    Dance and the Lived Body (1987)
Pittsburg, University of Pittsburg Press

Gaines, J. .    Fabrications Costumes and
and Herzog, C    the Female Body (1990)
London, Routledge

Guiraud, P.    Semiology (1975)
London, Routledge and Kegan Paul

Hall, E.T.    The Silent Language, New York (1982)
Doubleday

Humphrey, D.    The Art of Making Dances, New York (1959)
Reinhart & Co

Hutchinson Guest, A.    Your Move (1983)
London, Gordan and Breach

Jordan, S.    Striding Out (1992)
London, Dance Books

Jung, C.    Man and his Symbols (1964)
London, Aldus Books

Kirstein, L    The Classic Ballet (1977)
and Stuart, M.    London, A&C Black

Kostelanetz, R.    Merce Cunningham: Dancing in Space
and Time (1992)
Chicago, a Capella Books

**Laban, R.**
**ed. Ullmann. L.**

Mastery of Movement (1971)
London, Macdonald & Evans

Choreutics (1966)
London, Macdonald & Evans


**Lamb, W.**

Posture and Gesture (1965)
London, Duckworth


**Maletic, V.**

Body-Space-Expression (1987)
Berlin, de Gruyter


**Mumford, P.**

"Lighting Dance" (1985)
in Dance Theatre Journal Vol 3 No 2


**Nattiez, J.J.**

Music and Discourse (1970)
Princeton, Princeton University Press


**Nikolais, A.**

"Basic Dance and Sensory Perception" (1964)
in Dance Observer


**Pavis, P.**

Languages of the Stage (1993)
New York, Performing Arts Journal
Publication


**Preston-Dunlop, V.**

Dance Words (1995)
London, Harwood Academic Publishers

"Choreutic Concepts and Practice" (1983)
in Dance Research, Vol 1 No 1.


**Reid, F.**

Lighting the Stage (1995)
Oxford, Focal Press


**Reid, L.A.**

Ways of Understanding and Education (1986)
London, Heinemann


**Revill, D.**

The Roaring Silence: John Cage (1992)
London, Bloomsbury


**Shahn, B.**

The Shape of Content (1957)
Cambridge MA, Harvard University Press


**Sheets-Johnstone, M.**

The Phenomenology of Dance (1979)
London, Dance Books


**Siegel, M.**

The Shapes of Change: Images of
American Modern Dance (1972)
Boston, Houghton Mifflin

**Sorell, W.**                    Dance in Its Time (1981)
                                  New York, Anchor Press/Doubleday

**Teck, K.**                      Ear Training for the Body (1994)
                                  Pennington NJ, Dance Horizons

**Tufnell, M.
and Crickmay, C.**               Body Space Image (1988)
                                  London, Virago

# Valerie Preston-Dunlop

Valerie Preston-Dunlop's initial training in European Modern dance and ballet led to a career as a dancer, notator and teacher. After a pause for raising her family she returned to dance by studying for a Diploma in Education, an MA in Dance Studies and undertook practical and theoretical research for her doctorate. While retaining her interest in the roots of 20th Century European dance she focused on developing methods of dance study which married theory with practice. She is currently Research Fellow and Consultant at Trinity Laban in London.

**Dorothy Gifford Madden** is an internationally known teacher of choreography and author of 'You call me Louis, not Mr Horst' (1997). She founded Maryland Dance Theatre and the dance department of the University of Maryland of which she is a Professor Emerita.

**Glenn Hilling** who graduated in design from Middlesex Polytechnic is primarily involved with corporate and promotional design but his experience extends to other areas including exhibitions and interiors. He has also lectured in design at various Universities and Colleges.

**Angela Geary** trained at Glasgow School of Art, followed by a Masters degree in Conservation at the University of Northumbria. She is presently undertaking an MPhil in 3D computer imaging at the RCA. She is the Director of Conservation Services, a fine art restoration company.

# partial list of books by
# Valerie Preston-Dunlop

**Dance Words**                         New York and London,
                                        Harwood Academic Publishers (1995)

**Rudolf Laban:**                       London, Dance Books (1998)
**An Extraordinary Life**

**Schrifttanz:**                        London, Dance Books (1990)
**A View of German Dance**
**in the Weimar Republic**

**Point of Departure:**                 London, Verve Publishing (1984, 2008)
**The Dancer's Space**

**Dance and the Performative:**  London, Verve Publishing (2002, 2010)
**With Ana Sanchez Colberg**

**Rudolf Laban Man of Theatre:**  Dance Books (2013)

CPSIA information can be obtained
at www.ICGtesting.com
Printed in the USA
BVHW090304010219
539222BV00007B/147

9 781906 830700